Family
favorite recipes

Southern Supper Menu, page 309

Family
favorite recipes

Oxmoor House®

Family
favorite recipes

©2008 by Gooseberry Patch
600 London Road, Delaware, Ohio 43015
1-800-854-6673, www.gooseberrypatch.com
©2008 by Oxmoor House, Inc.
Book Division of Southern Progress Corporation
P. O. Box 2262, Birmingham, Alabama 35201-2262

Hardcover ISBN-13: 978-0-8487-3230-1
Hardcover ISBN-10: 0-8487-3230-8
Softcover ISBN-13: 978-0-8487-3251-6
Softcover ISBN-10: 0-8487-3251-0
Library of Congress Control Number: 2007941811
Printed in the United States of America
Second Printing 2008

Oxmoor House, Inc.
Editor in Chief: Nancy Fitzpatrick Wyatt
Executive Editor: Susan Payne Dobbs
Art Director: Keith McPherson
Managing Editor: Allison Long Lowery

Gooseberry Patch Family Favorite Recipes
Editor: Kelly Hooper Troiano
Project Editor: Diane Rose
Senior Designer: Emily Albright Parrish
Copy Chief: L. Amanda Owens
Editorial Assistant: Vanessa Rusch Thomas
Director, Test Kitchens: Elizabeth Tyler Austin
Assistant Director, Test Kitchens: Julie Christopher
Test Kitchens Professionals: Jane Chambliss; Patricia Michaud;
Kathleen Royal Phillips; Catherine Crowell Steele;
Ashley T. Strickland; Kate Wheeler, R.D.
Photography Director: Jim Bathie
Senior Photo Stylist: Kay E. Clarke
Associate Photo Stylist: Katherine G. Eckert
Director of Production: Laura Lockhart
Production Manager: Theresa Beste-Farley

Contributors
Designer: Amy R. Bickell
Compositor: Nancy Johnson
Copy Editor: Dolores Hydock
Proofreader: Lauren Brooks
Indexer: Mary Ann Laurens
Interns: Erin Loudy, Lauren Wiygul
Food Stylists: Ana Price Kelly, Debby Maugans
Photographers: Brian Francis, Beau Gustafson, Lee Harrelson
Photo Stylists: Leah Marlett, Katie Stoddard

To order additional publications, call 1-800-765-6400.

For more books to enrich your life, visit oxmoorhouse.com

To search, savor, and share thousands of recipes, visit myrecipes.com

Cover: Lasagna Rolls (page 77)

Dear Friend,

When you think of family favorites, do fond memories of Sunday dinners at Grandma's come to mind? Did you have a certain Friday-night treat? Was there a special birthday meal or dessert that was always a must-have? Family favorite foods can bring back recollections of sweet times spent with family & friends.

Virginia's Baked Spaghetti (page 73) is a recipe that was passed down from a reader's grandmother…who always used just a pinch of this and a dash of that. Lucky for us that this tasty spaghetti recipe was written down! The Best Salad (page 192) has been served every Thanksgiving and Christmas by another family since the 1960's…making this a tried & true dish that's been time-tested. And why not participate in the tradition of Good Neighbor Day? Surprise your neighbors on the fourth Sunday in September with gifts of Terrific Truffle Cake Mix (page 299).

As you take a look through the pages of *Family Favorite Recipes,* our newest book featuring our best-ever recipes, we hope you'll find some dishes that bring back fond memories and discover some new ones to share with your own family. Whether you're serving a family-style dinner of Dixie Fried Chicken (page 55) or baking up a batch of Happy Birthday Cookies (page 305) for a friend's special day, these delicious recipes will bring smiles and laughter…creating the sweetest memories of all.

Wishing you warm memories
& good food!

Vickie & JoAnn

contents

Antipasto, page 29

Mini Meat Loaves, page 123

9 Munchies & More
yummy appetizers, kid-friendly snacks & refreshing beverages

47 Memorable Main Dishes
special-occasion recipes

91 Fast Family Suppers
quick weeknight meals

131 Savory Sides
delicious side dishes for rounding out any meal

167 Soups, Sandwiches & Salads
scrumptious, tasty go-withs

205 Bountiful Breads
sweet & savory breads

Honey-Kissed Acorn Squash, page 159

Ice-Cream Tacos, page 237

233 Blue-Ribbon Desserts
sweet treats for everyone

273 Gifts from the Kitchen
homemade goodies for every occasion

306 Menus for All Seasons
16 fresh and seasonal menus

314 Handy Tips for Entertaining
easy how-to's for any get-together

317 Index
find any recipe…fast

320 How Did Gooseberry Patch
Get Started?
a story of two friends

Parmesan-Artichoke Crostini, page 34

munchies
& more

Appealing appetizers, kid-approved snacks and thirst-quenching beverages fill the pages of this party-pleasing chapter. Let Parmesan-Artichoke Crostini (page 34) be a part of your next gathering…this popular spread gets an update as a savory pick-up. Keep a stash of Grab 'n' Go Gorp (page 15) handy for a yummy and healthy snack. And for neighborly chats, whip up cupfuls of Hot Chocolate Supreme (page 13). Where these munchies are, you can bet you'll find family & friends!

Mexican coffee

Stir up this single-serving beverage as dessert after an evening meal…it's sure to satisfy any sweet tooth. The chocolate and hint of cinnamon give the coffee its Mexican origin.

1 c. hot, strong brewed coffee
1 T. grated semi-sweet chocolate
3 T. coffee liqueur

Whipped cream
Garnish: cinnamon stick

Combine first 3 ingredients in a large cup or mug; stir until chocolate melts. Dollop with whipped cream; garnish, if desired. Makes about 1¼ cups.

cup of cheer

Each fall, close friends and I get together for what we call our "Cup of Cheer." Though busy schedules keep us from gathering during the year, this special time gives us the opportunity to renew our friendships. It's a delightful afternoon spent enjoying tea, chatting and making memories. As a special keepsake, we exchange a teacup and saucer we've found at tag sales or antique shops during the past year. After five years of this cherished tradition, we each have a lovely and unique collection of teacups that reminds us of a special time with dear friends.

Delinda Blakney
Bridgeview, IL

spicy citrus cider

Keep this cider warm in a slow cooker…guests can help themselves.

8 c. apple juice
2¼ c. water
1½ c. orange juice
¼ c. molasses

1 T. whole cloves
3 (4-inch) cinnamon sticks
Garnish: apple slices

Combine all ingredients except apple slices in a large saucepan over medium heat. Simmer 10 minutes, stirring occasionally. Strain before serving. Garnish with apple slices, if desired. Makes about 3 quarts.

Ellen Folkman
Crystal Beach, FL

hot chocolate supreme

Curl up and enjoy a mug of this chocolatey cocoa on a frosty winter's day.

1 c. sugar
½ c. baking cocoa
¼ t. salt
5 c. water
2 c. milk

1 c. whipping cream
Garnishes: mini marshmallows or
    whipped topping, peppermint
    sticks

Combine sugar, cocoa and salt in a saucepan; whisk in water. Bring to a boil over high heat, stirring until sugar is completely dissolved. Reduce heat to medium; add milk and cream. Heat thoroughly and keep warm over low heat. If desired, serve topped with marshmallows or whipped topping and peppermint sticks. Makes 8¾ cups.

Lisa Allbright
Crockett, TX

cinnamon-sugar nuts

If you don't have a candy thermometer, try this simple test to know when your mixture has reached soft-ball stage: Drop a small amount of the candy mixture into cold water; the syrup will form a soft ball that flattens when removed from the water.

1 c. sugar
¼ c. evaporated milk
1 T. water
½ t. cinnamon

½ t. vanilla extract
⅛ t. salt
2¼ c. cashews

Combine sugar, evaporated milk, water, cinnamon, vanilla and salt in a saucepan. Bring to a boil over medium heat; boil until mixture reaches soft-ball stage, or 234 to 240 degrees on a candy thermometer.

Stir in cashews; turn out onto wax paper. Separate quickly using a fork. If nuts are stuck together after they cool, break them apart by hand. Store in an airtight container. Makes about 3 cups.

Kerry McNeil
Anacortes, WA

grab 'n' go gorp

Go ahead and dig into this merry mix of dried berries, chocolate and nuts…a perfect after-school snack. Or package it up into gifts or into single-serving snacks for lunch boxes.

2 c. crispy wheat cereal squares
2 c. mixed nuts
1 c. dried cherries
1 c. sweetened dried cranberries

1 c. dried blueberries
1 c. semi-sweet chocolate
   chips

Combine all ingredients in a large bowl; store in an airtight container. Makes 8 cups.

for parties...

Fill different baskets with dippers and snacks like pretzels, bagel chips, veggies, bread cubes and potato chips. Use a small riser (a book works well) to set under one side of the bottom of each basket to create a tilt…looks so nice, and guests can grab the food easily!

harvest moon caramel corn

Turn ordinary microwave popcorn into an extraordinary caramel snack. Not only is it good for movie night, but also it's a good treat for giving... especially since it makes an abundant amount!

10.5-oz. box microwave popcorn,
   popped
1 c. butter
2 c. brown sugar, packed

½ c. corn syrup
½ t. salt
1 t. vanilla extract
½ t. baking soda

Place popcorn in a lightly greased large roasting pan; set aside.

Combine butter, brown sugar, corn syrup and salt in a heavy saucepan. Bring to a boil over medium heat; cook 5 minutes. Remove from heat. Add vanilla and baking soda; stir well and pour over popcorn. Mix well.

Bake at 250 degrees for one hour, stirring occasionally. Let cool; break up and store in an airtight container. Makes 27 cups.

Kendra Guinn
Smithville, TN

"This treat is a family favorite during movie night at our home."

Kendra

celebration snack mix

Hail your favorite team's game day or the end of a school day as you munch on this smoky-flavored cereal and nut mix.

4 c. bite-size crispy corn cereal
   squares
4 c. bite-size crispy rice cereal
   squares
1 c. dry-roasted peanuts
1 c. mini pretzels
2 t. paprika
1 t. sugar

½ t. garlic salt
½ t. onion powder
¼ t. dry mustard
⅛ t. Cajun seasoning
3 T. canola oil
1½ t. Worcestershire sauce
½ t. smoke-flavored cooking
   sauce

Combine first 4 ingredients in a 2-gallon plastic zipping bag; set aside. Mix together paprika and next 5 ingredients in a small bowl; set aside. Combine oil and sauces; mix well and pour over cereal mixture. Close bag; shake gently until well coated. Gradually add spice mixture; close bag and shake until well coated. Store in an airtight container. Makes 8 cups.

Helen Woodard
Necedah, WI

snack containers

Use vintage canning jars to share snack mixes with friends & neighbors. Tie on bows and tags and you're all set...what could be easier?

Donna's party punch

With only three ingredients, this recipe will prove to be a party pleaser time and time again. Its red color makes this punch the perfect accompaniment for a Valentine's Day or Christmas party.

46-oz. can red fruit punch   1-ltr. bottle ginger ale, chilled
1 qt. raspberry sherbet, softened

   Mix together punch and sherbet; chill. Add ginger ale at serving time. Makes about 13 cups.

Linda Day
Wall, NJ

"This recipe is from a dear friend...it is so easy and tastes so good!"

Linda

cranberry slush

Create a festive garnish for each glass…just slip the cranberries and orange and lime slices onto wooden skewers.

¾ c. sugar
8 c. water, divided
2 c. white grape juice
12-oz. can frozen orange juice
  concentrate
12-oz. can frozen cranberry juice
  cocktail concentrate
6-oz. can frozen limeade
  concentrate
2-ltr. bottle lemon-lime soda, chilled
Garnishes: fresh cranberries, orange
  slices, lime slices

Combine sugar and 2 cups water in a large saucepan over medium heat, stirring until sugar dissolves. Add grape juice, next 3 ingredients and remaining 6 cups water. Pour into 2 (one-gallon-size) heavy-duty plastic zipping bags; freeze until solid. To serve, place frozen mixture into a punch bowl; pour chilled lemon-lime soda over mixture. Stir to break up chunks until mixture is slushy. Garnish each serving, if desired. Makes 23½ cups.

Judy Borecky
Escondido, CA

"Frozen grapes, strawberries and raspberries make flavorful ice cubes in frosty beverages. Freeze washed and dried fruit in a plastic zipping bag for up to three months…perfect for summer gatherings."

Gooseberry Patch

iced coffee

If you prefer a stronger coffee flavor, increase the amount of instant coffee granules to ¼ cup.

½ c. sugar
2 c. half-and-half
1 c. cold water
3 T. instant coffee granules

4 c. milk
¼ c. chocolate syrup
1 t. vanilla extract

Combine sugar and half-and-half in a large freezer-safe container. Combine water and coffee granules, stirring until granules dissolve; add to half-and-half mixture. Stir in milk, syrup and vanilla. Freeze 4 hours or until slushy. Makes 7 cups.

razzleberry tea

Sweet raspberries combine with tangy lemonade to make a fruity tea that's equally good served warm or chilled.

8 c. water, divided
5 regular-size tea bags
1¼ c. sugar
64-oz. bottle cranberry-raspberry
   juice, chilled

12-oz. pkg. frozen raspberries,
   thawed
12-oz. can frozen lemonade
   concentrate, thawed and divided

Bring 3 cups water to a boil in a saucepan. Remove from heat; add tea bags and let steep 8 minutes or until tea is desired strength. Discard tea bags.

While tea is warm, stir in sugar until dissolved; add enough of remaining water to equal 2 quarts. Pour tea into a large serving pitcher. Stir in juice, raspberries and half of the lemonade concentrate; save the remaining lemonade concentrate for another recipe. Serve warm or chilled. Makes 17¾ cups.

Susan deGraaff
Nicholasville, KY

a sweet gesture!

Sugar the rims of glasses before filling them with tea or punch. Just run a small lemon wedge around each rim and place the glass upside down on a small plate of sugar. Tap off any extra sugar before filling the glass.

garden-fresh salsa

Fresh-picked veggies from your garden or your local farmers' market really add flavor to homemade salsa. Offer no substitute here…store-bought salsa simply won't do!

14½-oz. can diced tomatoes, drained
¾ c. green pepper, diced
⅓ c. black olives, sliced
⅓ c. Spanish onion, diced
⅓ c. red onion, diced
2 T. fresh parsley, finely chopped
2 T. garlic, minced

1 T. fresh cilantro, finely chopped
1½ T. lemon juice
1 T. lime juice
2 plum tomatoes, diced
2 green onions, sliced
1 jalapeño pepper, diced
salt and pepper to taste

Combine all ingredients in a large bowl; refrigerate until ready to serve. Makes 4 cups.

Staci Meyers
Cocoa, FL

"I have added corn and black beans, too…you can't go wrong."

Staci

homemade tortilla chips

Make your own tortilla chips to go with salsas and dips…you won't believe how easy it is. Just slice flour tortillas into wedges, spray with non-stick vegetable spray and bake at 350 degrees for 5 to 7 minutes.

red pepper hummus

Roasted red peppers add variety and a splash of color to this classic Mediterranean dip.

15-oz. can chickpeas (garbanzo
    beans), drained
7-oz. jar roasted red peppers,
    drained
1 clove garlic

1 t. ground coriander
½ t. ground red pepper
¼ t. salt
pita chips or fresh vegetables

   Process all ingredients in a food processor until smooth. Store in an airtight container in the refrigerator up to one week. Serve with pita chips or fresh vegetables. Makes 1½ cups.

creative chip 'n' dip

   Prepare quick chip-n-dip sets in no time. Spoon dips into pottery soup bowls and set the bowls on top of dinner plates that hold crackers, veggies, pretzels, chips and bread.

Greek spread

Flavors of the Greek isles are found in this popular appetizer. Try preparing this spread in a shaped 2-quart mold for a bit of fun at your next get-together.

1 c. plus 1 T. almonds, chopped
  and divided
2 (8-oz.) pkgs. cream cheese,
  softened
10-oz. pkg. frozen spinach, thawed
  and drained

8-oz. pkg. feta cheese, crumbled
7-oz. jar roasted red peppers,
  drained and chopped
1 clove garlic, chopped
crackers or toasted pita wedges

Line a 2-quart bowl with plastic wrap; sprinkle with one tablespoon almonds. Mix together ½ cup almonds, cream cheese and next 4 ingredients in a separate mixing bowl; blend well. Press cream cheese mixture into prepared bowl over almonds. Cover and chill overnight.

Invert spread onto a serving dish. Remove plastic wrap; press remaining almonds onto the outside. Serve with crackers or pita wedges. Makes about 7 cups.

Stephanie Doyle
Lincoln University, PA

"A must for our parties... guests always request it!"

Stephanie

antipasto

Keep this recipe handy when you need something that's easy and can be made ahead. Serve with a slotted spoon or provide toothpicks for your guests.

16-oz. pkg. Cheddar cheese, cubed
16-oz. pkg. provolone cheese, cubed
16-oz. pkg. sliced mushrooms
1 lb. hard salami, cubed
½ lb. pepperoni, cubed
6-oz. can whole pitted ripe black
    olives, drained

1 onion, chopped
1 green pepper, chopped
1 jalapeño pepper, sliced
16-oz. bottle Italian salad dressing

Toss together all ingredients in a serving bowl. Cover and chill overnight. Makes 18 cups.

Doreen DeRosa
New Castle, PA

appealing skewers

When appetizers need to be served with skewers, think beyond toothpicks…try sprigs of rosemary, bamboo picks or sugar cane spears.

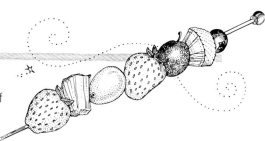

smoky salmon log

Keep this scrumptious spread on hand in the fridge…you'll be ready when surprise guests stop by!

2 c. canned salmon, drained and
    flaked
8-oz. pkg. cream cheese, softened
3 T. onion, chopped
1 T. lemon juice
1 t. prepared horseradish

¼ t. salt
¼ t. smoke-flavored cooking sauce
3 T. dried parsley
Optional: ½ c. pecans, chopped
Melba toast or assorted crackers

    Combine first 7 ingredients in a large bowl; mix well. Shape into a log; wrap in plastic wrap and chill. At serving time, roll in parsley and, if desired, pecans. Serve with toast or crackers. Makes about 4 cups.

Remona Putman
Rockwood, PA

creative cutouts

Use mini cookie cutters to cut toasted bread into charming shapes to serve alongside savory dips and spreads.

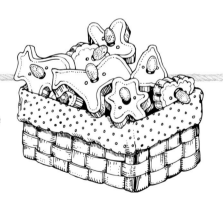

the cheesy bowl
(pictured on page 310)

Loaded with cheese and bacon, this appetizer is guaranteed to be a hands-down winner with your armchair quarterback! Light mayonnaise produces a creamier dip, so don't be tempted to substitute regular mayonnaise.

8-oz. block Colby-Jack cheese,
    shredded
1 c. shredded Parmesan cheese
2.8-oz. pkg. bacon bits

1½ c. light mayonnaise
½ c. onion, chopped
2 cloves garlic, minced
26-oz. round loaf bread

Stir together all ingredients except bread; set aside.

Hollow out bread, reserving torn pieces. Spoon dip into bread; place on an ungreased baking sheet. Bake at 350 degrees for one hour. Serve with torn bread or sliced apples. Makes 3½ cups.

Lisa Holdren
Wheeling, WV

"My relatives always ask me to bring this warm dip along to family gatherings. I like to serve it in a fragrant loaf of rosemary-olive oil bread from the bakery."

Lisa

apple & Brie toasts

A buttery mixture of brown sugar and chopped walnuts tops sweet apple slices and savory cheese for an elegant appetizer that will appeal to everyone. We used a combination of Granny Smith and Braeburn apples, but you can use your favorite. Fresh pears are a good option, too.

1 baguette, cut into ¼-inch-thick
    slices
½ c. brown sugar, packed
½ c. chopped walnuts
¼ c. butter, melted

13.2-oz. pkg. Brie cheese, thinly
    sliced
3 Granny Smith apples and/or
    Braeburn apples, cored and sliced

Arrange bread slices on an ungreased baking sheet; bake at 350 degrees until lightly toasted. Set aside.

Mix together sugar, walnuts and butter. Top each slice of bread with a cheese slice, an apple slice and one teaspoon of brown sugar mixture. Bake until cheese melts. Makes about 2½ dozen.

Jo Ann
Gooseberry Patch

"Everyone loves this!"

Jo Ann

Parmesan-artichoke crostini
(pictured on page 8)

We've taken the familiar (and popular) artichoke dip, jazzed it up with chopped green chiles and red peppers, then spread it over baguette slices. Save time by looking for toasted baguette slices in the supermarket bakery or substitute bagel chips or Melba toast rounds.

1 baguette
12-oz. jar marinated artichoke
    hearts, drained and chopped
4.5-oz. can chopped green chiles,
    drained

1 c. mayonnaise
1 c. shredded Parmesan
    cheese
¼ c. red pepper, finely chopped
2 cloves garlic, minced

Diagonally cut baguette into 42 (¼-inch-thick) slices. Reserve any remaining baguette for other uses. Arrange slices on large ungreased baking sheets. Broil slices one to 2 minutes or until toasted.

Stir together chopped artichoke hearts and next 5 ingredients.

Spread one tablespoon artichoke mixture on toasted side of each baguette slice.

Bake at 450 degrees for 6 to 7 minutes or until lightly browned and bubbly. Makes 3½ dozen.

tasty white spinach pizza

A prebaked crust gives you a jump start on this tasty pizza. With larger servings, this could be served as a main dish.

1 T. garlic, minced
2 T. olive oil
4 c. baby spinach, diced
12-inch prebaked Italian pizza crust
½ c. Alfredo sauce
8-oz. pkg. shredded mozzarella
    cheese, divided

1 c. grated Parmesan cheese,
    divided
Optional: sliced mushrooms, diced
    green olives with pimentos

Sauté garlic in oil in a large skillet over medium heat. Add spinach; cook until spinach wilts and absorbs oil. Remove from heat.

Place pizza crust on a lightly greased baking sheet; spread with Alfredo sauce. Sprinkle half the mozzarella and half the Parmesan over sauce. If desired, top with mushrooms and olives. Sprinkle remaining cheese over mushroom layer; top with spinach. Bake at 350 degrees for 15 to 20 minutes or until golden. Serves 6.

Mike Johnson
Columbus, OH

"My own creation...
a delicious change
from tomato-
based pizza."

Mike

fried cheese sticks

Just about everyone loves fried cheese sticks. Our version gets a punch of heat from ground red pepper and cheese spiced with jalapeños. To tame the heat, use plain Monterey Jack (without the peppers), mozzarella or Swiss cheese, and either omit the red pepper or use less of it.

2 (8-oz.) pkgs. Monterey Jack cheese
    with jalapeño peppers
1 c. all-purpose flour
1½ t. ground red pepper
1 c. fine, dry bread crumbs
1 t. dried parsley
4 eggs, beaten
vegetable oil
Optional: marinara sauce

Cut cheese crosswise into ¾-inch slices. Lay slices flat and cut in half lengthwise.

Combine flour and red pepper; stir well. Combine bread crumbs and parsley in another bowl; stir well. Dip cheese sticks in beaten eggs. Dredge in flour mixture. Dip coated cheese in egg again; dredge in bread crumb mixture, pressing firmly so that crumbs adhere. Place cheese sticks on a wax paper-lined baking sheet and freeze at least 30 minutes.

Fry cheese sticks in 375-degree deep oil until golden brown. Drain on paper towels. Serve immediately with marinara sauce, if desired. Makes 28 appetizers.

maple-topped sweet potato skins

Sweet potato skins offer a tasty alternative to regular potato skins. These are loaded with spices and topped with sugary walnuts...a savory-sweet side dish for any dinner.

6 large sweet potatoes
½ c. cream cheese, softened
¼ c. sour cream
2 t. cinnamon, divided
2 t. nutmeg, divided
2 t. ground ginger, divided

2 c. walnuts or pecans, chopped
¼ c. brown sugar, packed
3 T. butter, softened
Garnishes: maple syrup, apple slices,
    additional nuts

Pierce potatoes with a fork. Bake at 400 degrees for 45 minutes to one hour or microwave on high for 15 to 20 minutes or until tender; cool.

Slice each potato in half lengthwise; scoop out pulp, keeping skins intact. Mash pulp in a mixing bowl until smooth; add cream cheese, sour cream and one teaspoon each of spices. Mix well and spoon into potato skins. Stir together nuts, brown sugar, butter and remaining spices; sprinkle over top. Place potato skins on an ungreased baking sheet; bake at 400 degrees for 15 minutes. If desired, drizzle with warm syrup and garnish with apple slices and additional nuts. Serves 12.

Linda Corcoran
Metuchen, NJ

turkey-cranberry rolls

If you could put the taste of Thanksgiving in a sandwich, this would be it. Nothing could be easier than using prepackaged rolls that you slice, fill and then bake in the pan they came in. Since they freeze well, these rolls are good make-ahead sandwiches.

8-oz. pkg. cream cheese, softened

2 T. mayonnaise

2 T. sour cream

2 T. chutney

1 T. Dijon mustard

½ t. curry powder

½ t. ground red pepper

1 c. whole-berry cranberry sauce

3 T. onion, minced

4 (7½-oz.) pkgs. party rolls in
    aluminum trays

1 lb. smoked turkey, thinly sliced

Combine first 7 ingredients in a medium bowl. Beat at medium speed with an electric mixer until blended. Stir together cranberry sauce and onion.

Remove rolls from aluminum tray. Slice rolls in half horizontally, using a serrated knife; do not separate rolls. Spread a thin layer of cream cheese mixture over top and bottom halves of each package of rolls.

Layer one-fourth of the turkey slices over bottom half of each package of rolls. Spread a thin layer of cranberry mixture over turkey. Cover with top halves of rolls. Cut rolls into individual sandwiches and return rolls to aluminum trays.

Cover and bake at 350 degrees for 25 minutes or until warm. Bake, uncovered, during last 10 minutes, if desired, for crisper rolls. Makes 80 appetizers.

Greek olive cups

These tasty cups can be made ahead and frozen. Fill the cups in their trays, then place the trays in heavy-duty plastic zipping bags and freeze them up to one month. When ready to bake, remove the cups from their trays and place them on an ungreased baking sheet. Let the cups stand 10 minutes before baking. Bake as directed in the recipe.

1½ c. shredded Cheddar
   cheese, divided
½ c. pimento-stuffed olives or other
   green olives, chopped
½ c. kalamata olives, pitted and
   chopped

⅓ c. pecans, chopped and toasted
⅓ c. pine nuts, toasted
2½ T. mayonnaise
2 (2.1-oz.) pkgs. frozen mini phyllo
   shells

Combine one cup cheese and next 5 ingredients in a medium bowl. Remove phyllo shells from packages, leaving them in trays.

Spoon one heaping teaspoon olive mixture into each phyllo shell; sprinkle evenly with the remaining ½ cup cheese. Remove from trays and place cups on an ungreased baking sheet.

Bake at 375 degrees for 12 to 15 minutes or until thoroughly heated. Serve immediately. Makes 30 appetizers.

stack it up

Use tiered cake stands for bite-size appetizers…so handy, and they take up less space on the buffet table than setting out several serving platters.

blue-ribbon chicken fingers

Don't keep these chicken fingers just as an appetizer option. You'll want to serve them as a dinner entrée as well…you'll definitely get the thumbs-up!

6 boneless, skinless chicken breasts
1 c. milk
2 T. white vinegar
1 egg, beaten
1 t. garlic powder

1 c. all-purpose flour
1 c. seasoned bread crumbs
1 t. salt
1 t. baking powder
vegetable oil

Cut chicken into ½-inch strips; place in a large plastic zipping bag. Combine milk and vinegar in a small bowl; add egg and garlic powder. Pour milk mixture over chicken in bag; seal and refrigerate 4 to 6 hours.

Combine flour and next 3 ingredients in a separate plastic zipping bag. Drain chicken, discarding milk mixture. Place chicken in flour mixture; seal bag and shake to coat. Fry coated chicken strips in 375-degree deep oil 4 to 5 minutes on each side or until golden. Place on paper towels to drain. Serves 6 to 8.

Jackie Balla
Walbridge, OH

Asian gingered shrimp

Asian-style flavors make something special out of simple boiled shrimp. If you'd like to cook and peel your own shrimp, start with 3 pounds of raw shrimp in the shells.

1½ lbs. cooked, peeled and cleaned medium shrimp
¼ c. soy sauce
2 t. fresh ginger, peeled and finely chopped

¼ c. white vinegar
2 T. sugar
2 T. sweet sake or apple juice
1½ t. salt
2 to 3 T. green onions, thinly sliced

Arrange shrimp in a single layer in a shallow glass container; set aside.

Bring soy sauce to a boil in a small saucepan; add ginger. Reduce heat and simmer 5 minutes or until most of liquid is absorbed. Stir in vinegar, sugar, sake or apple juice and salt; pour over shrimp. Cover with plastic wrap; refrigerate 2 hours to overnight.

Remove shrimp from marinade with a slotted spoon; arrange on a serving platter. Sprinkle with green onions. Serves 8 to 10.

Lynn Williams
Muncie, IN

"Serve with steamed rice for a delicious main dish."

Lynn

bacon-wrapped scallops

Wrapped in bacon strips, these succulent scallops will be snapped up quickly! Be sure to buy sea scallops, which are larger in diameter than the smaller bay scallops.

11 bacon slices, cut in half
½ c. all-purpose flour
1½ t. paprika
½ t. salt
½ t. ground white pepper
½ t. garlic powder

1 c. milk
1 egg
22 sea scallops
1 to 2 c. Japanese bread crumbs
   (panko)
Rémoulade Sauce

Cook bacon slices 3 to 4 minutes or until translucent.

Combine flour and next 4 ingredients in a shallow dish. Beat together milk and egg in a small bowl. Roll scallops in seasoned flour, shaking off excess. Dip scallops in egg mixture, then coat with bread crumbs.

Wrap each scallop with bacon and secure with a toothpick. Place scallops on a lightly greased baking sheet. Bake at 400 degrees for about 30 minutes or until bacon is crisp and scallops are cooked. Serve hot with Rémoulade Sauce. Serves 11.

rémoulade sauce:

½ c. celery, minced
½ c. green onions, minced
½ c. mayonnaise
½ c. cocktail sauce
¼ c. prepared mustard
¼ c. horseradish

¼ c. lemon juice
¼ c. red wine vinegar
2 t. paprika
1 t. salt
½ t. pepper
⅛ t. ground red pepper

Mix together all ingredients in a quart jar; shake well and chill 45 minutes. Makes 2¼ cups.

Robyn Wright
Delaware, OH

"This is an elegant and tasty appetizer for a New Year's Eve gathering!"

Robyn

Beef in Rosemary-Mushroom
Sauce, page 80

memorable
main dishes

If you're searching for that perfect dish for a birthday celebration, hearty servings of Italian 3-Cheese Stuffed Shells (page 75) are sure to satisfy partygoers, and for the big holiday feast, savory Roast Turkey with Sage Butter (page 63) will bring smiles to the faces of your guests. Check out these and other scrumptious recipes in this chapter to fit your special occasion.

seafood lasagna

Chock-full of shrimp, scallops and crab meat, this creamy lasagna is a dream come true for seafood lovers.

1 c. onion, chopped
5 large cloves garlic, divided
¼ c. butter, divided
3 T. all-purpose flour
¼ t. salt
½ t. pepper
3 c. milk
8-oz. pkg. cream cheese, cut into
   cubes
1 c. grated Parmesan cheese,
   divided

½ lb. medium shrimp, peeled,
   cleaned and cooked
8 oz. bay scallops, cooked
16-oz. bag frozen cut-leaf spinach
1 lb. mushrooms, chopped
1 T. olive oil
18 lasagna noodles, cooked in salted
   water
1 lb. crab meat
4 c. shredded mozzarella cheese

Sauté onion and 3 cloves garlic in 3 tablespoons butter in a 3-quart sauce-pan over medium heat until tender. Whisk in flour, salt and pepper until smooth. Gradually whisk in milk. Cook, whisking constantly, until thickened and smooth. Whisk in cream cheese and ½ cup Parmesan cheese until cream cheese melts and sauce is smooth. Reserve one cup sauce. Stir shrimp and scallops into remaining sauce; set aside.

Prepare spinach according to package directions. Sauté mushrooms and remaining 2 cloves garlic in remaining one tablespoon butter and olive oil until tender. Stir in spinach; drain.

Spread reserved one cup sauce in a thin layer on the bottom of a lightly greased 15"x10" lasagna dish. Layer 6 lasagna noodles over sauce. Spread one-third of seafood sauce over noodles; top with half of spinach mixture, half of crab and one cup mozzarella cheese. Repeat layers. Layer remaining 6 noodles and remaining one-third of seafood sauce over mozzarella cheese. Top with remaining ½ cup Parmesan cheese and remaining 2 cups mozzarella cheese. Bake, uncovered, at 350 degrees for 40 minutes or until bubbly. Let stand 10 minutes before serving. Serves 12.

Christi Miller
New Paris, PA

coconut shrimp

Coated with shredded coconut and then fried, these golden gems are good!
Garnish with fresh orange slices, if desired.

1½ c. canola oil
1 c. all-purpose flour
1 c. beer

1 lb. uncooked medium shrimp,
    peeled and cleaned
14-oz. pkg. shredded coconut

Pour oil into a large skillet and heat oil to 375 degrees. Stir together flour
and beer. Coat shrimp with batter, then roll in coconut. Fry shrimp in small
batches about 2 to 3 minutes until golden and curled. Drain on paper towels.
Serves 4.

eye-catching arrangements

It's easy to make oh-so-pretty floral arrangements by
using unexpected containers. Instead of vases, try stand-
ing flowers in jars of water, then tuck the jars into simple
shopping bags, formal top hats or vintage purses.

shrimp & wild rice

To save time, have the seafood department steam the shrimp for you. They'll need to start with ¾ pound of unpeeled raw shrimp.

6-oz. pkg. long-grain and wild rice
    mix, uncooked
1 yellow onion, chopped
1 green pepper, chopped
½ c. butter
8-oz. pkg. sliced mushrooms

1 t. hot pepper sauce
salt and pepper to taste
1 c. heavy cream
½ lb. cooked, peeled and cleaned
    medium shrimp
¼ c. slivered or sliced almonds

Prepare wild rice mix according to package directions.

Sauté onion and green pepper in butter in a large skillet until tender. Add mushrooms, hot pepper sauce and salt and pepper to taste; remove from heat. Add cream and rice; cool slightly. Add shrimp, mixing well, and pour into a buttered 11"x 7" baking dish; top with almonds. Bake, uncovered, at 350 degrees for 30 minutes. Serves 4.

Teresa Mulhern
Powell, OH

"I've used this many times for potlucks and have never had to bring home leftovers! It's also a great main dish served with salad and bread!"

Teresa

linguine & white clam sauce

Canned clams are given a flavorful boost when combined with a creamy sauce and served over linguine.

2 (6½-oz.) cans minced clams,
   drained and juices reserved
milk
½ c. onion, finely chopped
1 clove garlic, minced
2 T. butter
¼ c. all-purpose flour

½ t. dried oregano
½ t. salt
¼ t. pepper
¼ c. sherry or chicken broth
2 T. dried parsley
8-oz. pkg. linguine, cooked
½ c. grated Parmesan cheese

Combine reserved clam juice with enough milk to equal 2 cups liquid; set aside.

Cook onion and garlic in butter in a medium saucepan over medium heat until tender and golden; stir in flour. Add clam juice mixture to pan; stir over low heat until smooth. Add oregano, salt and pepper; cook until thick and bubbly, stirring frequently. Stir in clams and sherry or chicken broth; cook one more minute. Sprinkle with parsley and stir. Toss with cooked linguine; sprinkle with Parmesan cheese. Serves 4.

Kristie Rigo
Friedens, PA

lime & ginger grilled salmon

(pictured on page 308)

This salmon not only tastes good…it's good for you as well. Eat up and enjoy!

2-lb. salmon fillet, cleaned and
   boned
2 T. fresh ginger, peeled and minced
2 T. lime zest

½ t. salt
½ t. pepper
2 T. butter, melted, or olive oil
½ t. lime juice

Preheat grill to medium-high heat (350 to 400 degrees). Sprinkle salmon with ginger, lime zest, salt and pepper. Combine butter or olive oil and lime juice in a small bowl; brush salmon with mixture. Grill about 5 minutes on each side or until salmon flakes easily with a fork. Serves 4.

a special touch

When serving seafood, wrap lemon halves in cheesecloth, tie with colorful ribbon and set one on each plate. Guests can squeeze the lemon over their food…the cheesecloth prevents squirting and catches seeds!

Dixie fried chicken

Fried chicken is comfort food at its best! And this crispy Southern-style chicken, complete with a creamy gravy doesn't disappoint.

2½- to 3-lb. broiler-fryer, cut up, or
   2½ lbs. assorted chicken pieces
½ t. salt
½ t. freshly ground black pepper
1½ c. all-purpose flour

1 t. ground red pepper
1 egg, lightly beaten
⅓ c. milk
vegetable oil
Cream Gravy

Season chicken with salt and black pepper. Combine flour and red pepper; set aside. Combine egg and milk; dip chicken in egg mixture and dredge in flour mixture, coating chicken well. Pour oil to a depth of one inch in a heavy 10" to 12" skillet; heat oil to 350 degrees. Fry chicken in hot oil over medium heat 15 to 20 minutes or until golden, turning occasionally. Remove small pieces earlier, if necessary, to prevent overbrowning. Drain chicken on paper towels, reserving ¼ cup drippings in skillet for Cream Gravy. Serve with gravy. Serves 4.

cream gravy:

¼ c. reserved pan drippings
¼ c. all-purpose flour
2½ to 3 c. hot milk

½ t. salt
¼ t. freshly ground black pepper
dash of ground red pepper

Heat pan drippings in skillet over medium heat. Add flour, stirring until browned. Gradually add hot milk; cook, stirring constantly, until thick and bubbly. Add salt, black pepper and red pepper. Serve hot. Makes 2¾ cups.

holiday traditions

Every 4th of July was an event for our family. Mother made fried chicken, salads and all the trimmings, and Dad was in charge of the fireworks. Grandpa brought everything needed for root beer floats, and we could have as many as our tummies could hold!

Sylvia Mathews
Vancouver, WA

garlic & lemon roasted chicken
(pictured on page 308)

Roasted potatoes and baby carrots make this chicken a satisfying one-dish meal...delicious!

4-lb. roasting chicken	¼ c. butter, softened
½ t. salt	1 lemon, halved
½ t. freshly ground black pepper	3 T. water
½ t. dried parsley	1 lb. potatoes, peeled and cubed
7 cloves garlic	2 c. baby carrots

Place chicken on a lightly greased rack in a 13"x9" roasting pan. Combine salt, pepper, parsley, 2 cloves pressed garlic and one tablespoon butter; rub over chicken. Squeeze lemon halves over chicken. Place lemon halves, remaining 5 cloves garlic, halved, and remaining 3 tablespoons butter inside chicken cavity. Tie ends of legs together with string.

Pour water into roasting pan. Cover pan tightly with aluminum foil, making sure foil doesn't touch top of chicken. Bake at 375 degrees for 20 minutes. Add potatoes and carrots to pan. Bake, uncovered, 40 to 60 more minutes or until a meat thermometer inserted into thigh registers 170 degrees, basting occasionally with pan juices. Serves 4 to 6.

Terry Esposito
Freehold, NJ

honeymoon chicken & biscuits

Quick-cooking oats and maple syrup are the "secret" ingredients in the biscuits you'll find atop this chicken casserole.

1 c. red onion, chopped
½ c. butter, divided
10½-oz. can chicken broth
¼ c. dry sherry or water
1 c. all-purpose flour, divided
1 t. poultry seasoning
2½ c. chopped cooked chicken
    breast

10-oz. pkg. frozen vegetables
    (mushrooms, corn, carrots,
    peas, green beans)
¾ c. quick-cooking oats
2 t. baking powder
½ c. fat-free milk
1 egg white
1 T. maple syrup

Cook onion in 2 tablespoons butter in a large skillet over medium-high heat 3 minutes or until tender. Stir together broth, sherry or water, ¼ cup flour and seasoning; add to skillet. Cook 3 minutes or until thickened. Stir in chicken and vegetables; pour into a lightly greased 2-quart baking dish.

Combine remaining ¾ cup flour, oats and baking powder. Cut in remaining 6 tablespoons butter until crumbly. Stir in milk, egg white and syrup until moistened. Drop by ¼ cupfuls onto chicken. Bake at 425 degrees for 35 to 40 minutes. Serves 6.

Carol Blessing
Cropseyville, NY

tickled pink!

Many times our church had dinner outside. There were several tables loaded with made-from-scratch food. Granny would always bring the chicken & dumplings, which were the best in the world. Sometimes she would add just a drop of yellow food coloring to the dumplings for some color, but once she added red by mistake! Even though the chicken & dumplings were pink and there were lots of laughs, the wonderful taste was still the same!

Robin Wilson
Altamonte Springs, FL

"My husband's 80-year-old grandmother had lots of cooking advice for me and watched me like a hawk in the kitchen. One day I made this dish while she was out. That night Grandma ate with wild abandon! There wasn't a trace of food left on her plate! She's 88 now and never fails to request this dish whenever she visits."

Carol

gift-wrapped chicken

Good things come in small packages...like these chicken breasts layered in the middle with cranberry sauce and wrapped in phyllo dough. These goodies turn an ordinary meal into something extraordinary.

4 boneless, skinless chicken breasts
½ t. salt
¼ t. pepper
¼ c. whole-berry cranberry
  sauce

¼ c. butter
½ (16-oz.) pkg. phyllo dough,
  thawed
½ c. butter, melted

Cut each chicken breast in half the short way and pound each piece to flatten slightly; sprinkle with salt and pepper. Place one tablespoon cranberry sauce and one tablespoon unmelted butter on each of 4 pieces of chicken breast and place another breast piece on top.

Unroll dough and cut dough in half lengthwise. Working with 8 strips of dough at a time, stack 2 strips together for a total of 4 stacks. (Keep remaining phyllo covered with a damp towel to prevent drying out.) Brush each stack with melted butter. To make a package, layer 2 sets of stacks to make an "x," then layer remaining 2 sets of stacks on top to form a "t." Place filled chicken in center of dough stack and pull ends up together in the center, pinching ends closed at the top like a beggar's purse. Place on a greased baking sheet. Repeat procedure with remaining ingredients. Bake at 375 degrees for 30 minutes. Shield tops with aluminum foil during last 10 minutes of baking, if necessary. Serves 4.

The Governor's Inn
Ludlow, VT

"We think this makes a beautiful presentation...just like a package!"

Gooseberry Patch

Italian stuffed chicken

This is good! Sautéed mushrooms and Italian bread crumbs combine with three types of cheese to make the flavorful stuffing for these chicken breasts.

8-oz. pkg. sliced mushrooms
2 T. butter
1 c. ricotta cheese
1 c. shredded mozzarella cheese
½ c. grated Parmesan cheese

¼ c. dried parsley
¼ c. Italian-seasoned dry bread crumbs
4 bone-in chicken breasts
paprika

Sauté mushrooms in butter in a skillet over medium heat until tender; set aside. Combine cheeses, parsley and bread crumbs; mix well. Stir into mushroom mixture.

Loosen skin from chicken breasts without detaching it. Spoon mixture underneath skin; sprinkle with paprika. Arrange chicken in a lightly greased 13"x9" baking dish. Bake at 350 degrees for one hour and 7 minutes or until chicken is done. Serves 4.

Kathy Solka
Ishpeming, MI

maple-glazed turkey breast

Sprinkle in some sweetened dried cranberries for an extra burst of color and flavor.

6-oz. pkg. long-grain and wild rice
   mix, uncooked
1¼ c. water
1-lb. turkey breast

¼ c. maple syrup
½ c. chopped walnuts
½ t. cinnamon

Mix together rice mix, seasoning packet from rice mix and water in a 4-quart slow cooker. Place turkey breast, skin-side up, on rice mixture. Drizzle with syrup; sprinkle with walnuts and cinnamon.

Cover and cook on low setting 4 to 5 hours or until a meat thermometer inserted into breast registers 165 degrees. Let stand 10 minutes before slicing. Serves 4.

Eleanor Paternoster
Bridgeport, CT

kitchen journal

Jot down favorite recipes and family members' preferences in a kitchen journal. It'll make meal planning a snap!

roast turkey with sage butter

Any meal is a special occasion when this roasted turkey is the centerpiece of your menu. A luscious sage butter is used for seasoning, basting and serving your turkey.

1 c. butter, softened
3 T. fresh sage, chopped
8 slices bacon, crisply cooked and
    crumbled
salt and pepper to taste
16-lb. turkey, thawed if frozen

3 c. leeks, chopped
8 sprigs fresh sage
3 bay leaves, crumbled
4 c. chicken broth, divided
Garnishes: fresh sage sprigs,
    crabapples, pears

Combine butter, sage and bacon in a medium bowl; sprinkle lightly with salt and pepper. Set aside.

Remove giblets and neck from thawed turkey; reserve for another use. Rinse turkey and pat dry. Sprinkle inside of turkey with salt and pepper; add leeks, sage sprigs and bay leaves. Loosen skin and spread ⅓ cup butter mixture over breast meat under skin. Place turkey on the rack of a large broiler pan. Rub 2 tablespoons butter mixture on outside of turkey. Set aside ⅓ cup butter mixture for gravy; reserve remaining butter mixture for basting. Pour ⅓ cup broth over turkey.

Bake turkey at 350 degrees for about 2½ hours or until a meat thermometer inserted into thigh registers at least 170 degrees, shielding if necessary to prevent overbrowning. Baste turkey every 30 minutes with ⅓ cup broth; brush occasionally with remaining butter mixture. Transfer turkey to a platter; keep warm. Let stand 30 minutes.

To make gravy, pour pan juices and golden bits from roasting pan into a large glass measuring cup. Spoon off fat and discard. Bring juices and 2 cups broth to a boil over high heat in a large saucepan; boil until liquid is reduced to 2 cups, about 6 minutes. Whisk in reserved ⅓ cup butter mixture. Season with pepper. Garnish with sage, crabapples and pears, if desired. Serve turkey with gravy. Serves 12.

Kendall Hale
Lynn, MA

"An all-American dish that's perfect for your harvest table."

Kendall

savory turkey loaf

Not your ordinary meatloaf! Grated apple keeps it moist.

1 t. canola oil
1 c. onion, chopped
1 rib celery, chopped
¾ t. dried thyme
½ t. dried sage
1½ lbs. ground turkey
1½ c. bread crumbs
1½ c. apple, cored, peeled and
   grated

1 egg, beaten
2 T. fresh parsley, chopped
1 T. mustard
¾ t. salt
½ t. pepper
Glaze

Heat oil in a skillet over medium-high heat. Add onion and celery; sauté about 3 minutes. Stir in thyme and sage. Cool slightly.

Combine ground turkey, onion mixture, bread crumbs and next 6 ingredients in a bowl; mix well. Shape into a loaf; place in a greased 8"x4" loaf pan.

Bake, uncovered, at 350 degrees for one hour. Drain drippings from pan; brush Glaze over top of loaf. Return to oven; bake about 10 to 15 more minutes until top is golden or until a meat thermometer inserted into thickest portion registers 160 degrees. Serves 6 to 8.

glaze:

2 T. brown sugar, packed
2 T. cider vinegar

2 t. mustard

Stir together all ingredients in a bowl until brown sugar dissolves. Makes about ¼ cup.

Kim Hill-DeGroot
Macomb Township, MI

maple-curry pork roast
(pictured on page 310)

Pure maple syrup in the pork marinade hints of the flavors of fall.

1½ lbs. pork tenderloin
½ c. maple syrup
2 T. soy sauce
2 T. catsup
1 T. Dijon mustard

1½ t. curry powder
1½ t. ground coriander
1 t. Worcestershire sauce
2 cloves garlic, minced

Place pork in a large, heavy-duty plastic zipping bag; set aside. Whisk together syrup and next 7 ingredients in a medium bowl. Pour over pork; refrigerate at least one hour.

Transfer pork with marinade to an ungreased 13"x9" baking pan. Bake, uncovered, at 350 degrees for 35 minutes or until a meat thermometer inserted into thickest portion registers 155 degrees. Let stand, covered, 10 minutes or until thermometer registers 160 degrees. Thinly slice and drizzle with sauce from pan. Serves 6.

Sharon Demers
Dolores, CO

"This is wonderful on a cool fall day served with oven-roasted root vegetables, homemade applesauce and sweet potato biscuits."

Sharon

Sunday pork roast

Simple ingredients enhance the flavors of this roast for a meal special enough for Sunday dinner.

3 cloves garlic, minced
1 T. dried rosemary
salt and pepper to taste

2-lb. boneless pork loin roast
2 T. olive oil
½ c. white wine or chicken broth

Crush garlic with rosemary, salt and pepper. Pierce pork with a sharp knife tip in several places and press half the garlic mixture into openings. Rub pork with remaining garlic mixture and olive oil. Place pork in a lightly greased 13"x9" baking pan.

Bake, uncovered, at 350 degrees for one hour and 15 minutes or until a meat thermometer inserted into thickest portion registers 155 degrees. Let stand, covered, 10 minutes or until thermometer registers 160 degrees. Remove to a serving platter; slice and keep warm. Add wine or broth to pan, stirring to loosen browned bits. Serve pan drippings over pork. Serves 6 to 8.

Tiffany Brinkley
Broomfield, CO

"Arrange pork slices over mashed potatoes for a farm-style meal that's so hearty and filling."

Tiffany

autumn pork with apple chutney

A bold dry rub coats these tenderloins as they bake. Then they're served with a chutney full of apples, raisins, ginger and pecans...perfect for an autumn evening meal.

1 clove garlic, minced
1 T. ground ginger
1 T. mustard seed
1½ t. red pepper flakes
1 t. allspice

1 t. fennel seed
1 t. dried thyme
2 (1-lb.) pork tenderloins
Chutney

Process garlic and seasonings in a blender until ground to a powder. Coat pork with powder. Place pork in a lightly greased shallow roasting pan.

Bake at 450 degrees for 20 to 25 minutes or until a meat thermometer inserted into thickest portion registers 155 degrees. Let stand, covered, 10 minutes or until thermometer registers 160 degrees. To serve, slice pork into ½-inch medallions and top with Chutney. Serve remaining Chutney on the side. Serves 6.

chutney:

1 apple, cored, peeled and chopped
¾ c. fennel, diced
¾ c. brown sugar, packed
½ c. cider vinegar

⅓ c. raisins
1 T. crystallized ginger, chopped
½ t. salt
¼ c. chopped pecans

Combine first 7 ingredients in a medium saucepan; mix well. Bring mixture to a boil. Reduce heat to low; cover and cook 15 minutes. Remove cover and cook 15 to 20 more minutes or until fruit is tender. Stir in pecans. Makes 2 cups.

Jo Ann
Gooseberry Patch

pork chops supreme

A creamy sauce tops these slow-cooked, tender chops to make them superior.

6 pork chops
paprika to taste
salt and pepper to taste
2 T. olive oil
1 c. water
½ c. celery, chopped

1½-oz. pkg. onion soup mix
2 T. all-purpose flour
1 T. fresh parsley, chopped
¼ c. cold water
6-oz. can evaporated milk

Sprinkle pork chops with paprika, salt and pepper. Brown chops slowly in hot oil in a large skillet over medium heat; drain off excess oil. Add water, celery and onion soup mix. Cover and cook over low heat 45 minutes or until chops are tender. Remove chops from pan and place on a platter.

In a small bowl, combine flour, parsley and cold water; mix until smooth. Whisk into pan drippings, adding evaporated milk. Cook and stir until sauce is thick and bubbly, about 2 to 3 minutes. Cover chops with sauce. Serves 6.

Sharon Pawlak
Castle Rock, CO

"These pork chops are terrific served with rice, mashed potatoes or pasta."

Sharon

handwritten menus

These lend a personal touch to any table. Cut colored papers to fit the front of old-fashioned milk bottles or Mason jars. Write the details on them and wrap them around the jars with a pretty ribbon…fill jars with water and flowers and arrange in the center of the table.

farmhouse pork & cabbage sauté

Coleslaw, apples and potatoes are cooked with these golden chops for a hearty, warming one-dish dinner.

4 bone-in pork loin chops
¾ t. salt, divided
¼ t. pepper, divided
6 slices bacon, crisply cooked,
   crumbled and drippings reserved
1 onion, thinly sliced
16-oz. pkg. shredded coleslaw mix

2 Golden Delicious apples, cored
   and sliced
¾ lb. redskin potatoes, cubed
¾ c. apple cider
¼ t. dried thyme
1 T. cider vinegar

Sprinkle pork chops with ¼ teaspoon salt and ⅛ teaspoon pepper; set aside. Heat reserved bacon drippings in a Dutch oven over medium-high heat. Cook chops about 8 minutes or until golden on both sides and nearly done. Remove chops to a plate; keep warm.

Add onion to pan. Cover and cook over medium heat 8 minutes or until tender and golden, stirring occasionally. Gradually stir in coleslaw mix; cook about 5 minutes or until wilted. Add apples, potatoes, cider, thyme and remaining salt and pepper; bring to a boil. Reduce heat; cover and simmer 15 to 20 minutes or until potatoes are tender. Stir in vinegar; return chops to pan and heat thoroughly. Sprinkle with bacon. Serves 4.

Jo Ann
Gooseberry Patch

praline mustard-glazed ham
(pictured on page 307)

A savory raisin sauce with sliced apples glazes this spiral-cut ham.

7- to 8-lb. bone-in, smoked
    spiral-cut ham half
1 c. maple syrup
¾ c. brown sugar, packed
¾ c. Dijon mustard

⅓ c. apple juice
½ c. raisins
1 Granny Smith apple, cored,
    peeled and thinly sliced

Remove and discard skin and any excess fat from ham. Place in a lightly greased 13"x9" baking pan; insert a meat thermometer into thickest part of ham. Combine syrup, brown sugar, mustard and apple juice; pour over ham. Set pan on lowest oven rack. Bake at 350 degrees, basting with drippings every 20 minutes for 2½ hours or until a meat thermometer inserted into thickest portion of ham registers 140 degrees. Let ham stand for 10 minutes; remove from pan to a platter, reserving drippings.

To make sauce, heat drippings with raisins and apple slices in a small saucepan over low heat 5 minutes. Serve sliced ham with warm sauce. Serves 12.

Sheri Dulaney
Englewood, OH

Virginia's baked spaghetti

A favorite like this cheesy spaghetti casserole is a perfect choice for a family dinner or to take along to a potluck.

16-oz. pkg. spaghetti noodles,
    cooked
2 (24-oz.) jars spaghetti sauce
2 lbs. ground beef, browned
¼ c. butter
¼ c. all-purpose flour

¼ c. grated Parmesan cheese
2 t. salt
½ t. garlic powder
12-oz. can evaporated milk
3 c. shredded sharp Cheddar
    cheese, divided

Combine spaghetti noodles, spaghetti sauce and ground beef in a large bowl; set aside. Melt butter in a saucepan over medium heat; add flour, Parmesan cheese, salt and garlic powder, stirring constantly until smooth and bubbly. Add evaporated milk and one cup Cheddar cheese; stir until thickened.

Pour half of spaghetti noodle mixture into a greased 13"x9" casserole dish and pour cheese mixture over top. Pour remaining noodle mixture into dish; top with remaining 2 cups Cheddar cheese. Bake at 350 degrees for 25 to 30 minutes. Serves 12.

Mindy Beard
Yorktown, IN

"This is my husband's grandma's recipe. She loved to bake and cook but rarely used a recipe...it came straight from her heart! I am so fortunate to have written this one down."

Mindy

kids' table

Make the kids' table fun! Use a sheet of butcher paper for the tablecloth; place a flowerpot filled with markers, crayons and stickers in the middle...they'll have a blast!

Draw Here!

Italian 3-cheese stuffed shells

Stuffed pasta shells have never been as good as these, which are filled with three types of cheese and zesty Italian flavors.

1 lb. ground chuck
1 c. onion, chopped
1 clove garlic, minced
2 c. hot water
12-oz. can tomato paste
1 T. instant beef bouillon granules
1½ t. dried oregano

16-oz. container cottage cheese
8-oz. pkg. shredded mozzarella
   cheese, divided
½ c. grated Parmesan cheese
1 egg, beaten
24 jumbo pasta shells, cooked

Cook beef, onion and garlic in a large skillet over medium-high heat, stirring until beef crumbles and is no longer pink; drain. Stir in water, tomato paste, bouillon granules and oregano; simmer over medium heat about 30 minutes.

Stir together cottage cheese, one cup mozzarella, Parmesan cheese and egg in a medium bowl; mix well. Stuff cooked shells with cheese mixture; arrange in a greased 13"x9" baking pan. Pour beef mixture over shells. Cover and bake at 350 degrees for 40 to 45 minutes. Uncover and sprinkle with remaining mozzarella cheese. Bake 5 more minutes or until cheese melts. Serves 6 to 8.

Melanie McNew
Cameron, MO

"A super dish for any get-together, and it's so simple to whip up."

Melanie

stuffed cabbage rolls

You get your meat and veggies all rolled up in one entrée.

12 leaves cabbage
1¼ lbs. ground beef
1 c. cooked rice
1 onion, chopped
1 egg, beaten
½ t. poultry seasoning or
  dried thyme

2 T. canola oil
2 (8-oz.) cans tomato sauce
1 T. brown sugar, packed
¼ c. water
1 T. lemon juice or vinegar

Cover cabbage leaves with boiling water; let stand 5 minutes or until leaves are limp. Drain and set aside.

Combine ground beef, rice, onion, egg and poultry seasoning or thyme; mix well. Place equal portions of meat mixture in center of each cabbage leaf. Fold sides of each leaf over meat mixture; roll up and fasten with a toothpick.

Heat oil in a large skillet over medium heat; add rolls and sauté until golden. Pour tomato sauce into skillet. Combine brown sugar, water and lemon juice or vinegar; stir into tomato sauce. Cover and simmer one hour, basting occasionally. Serves 6.

Alexis Mauriello
Richardson, TX

lasagna rolls
(pictured on cover)

Double this casserole so you can have one to keep and one to either give away or freeze for holiday company…it freezes for up to one month.

11 lasagna noodles, uncooked
1 lb. Italian sausage, casing removed
1 small onion, chopped
1 clove garlic, minced
26-oz. jar spaghetti sauce
¼ c. dry white wine or chicken broth
3 T. fresh parsley, chopped
½ t. salt

3 c. ricotta cheese
1 c. shredded mozzarella cheese
2 eggs, lightly beaten
⅓ c. fine, dry bread crumbs
2 T. grated Parmesan cheese
1 t. Italian seasoning
½ c. grated Parmesan cheese

Cook lasagna noodles according to package directions; drain. Cut in half crosswise and set aside.

Cook sausage, onion and garlic in a large skillet, stirring until sausage crumbles and is no longer pink; drain. Add spaghetti sauce, wine or broth, parsley and salt, stirring well. Cover and simmer 10 minutes, stirring occasionally. Remove from heat and set aside.

Combine ricotta cheese and next 5 ingredients, stirring well. Spread ricotta mixture evenly over lasagna noodles. Roll up jelly-roll fashion, starting at narrow end. Place lasagna rolls, seam-side down, in a lightly greased 13"x9" baking dish. Pour meat sauce over rolls and sprinkle with ½ cup Parmesan cheese. Bake, covered, at 375 degrees for 30 minutes. Uncover and bake 15 more minutes or until thoroughly heated. Serves 8 to 10.

Mexican lasagna

We give lasagna a Mexican flavor in this recipe. Corn tortillas take
lasagna noodles; Cheddar and Monterey Jack cheese replace moz
chopped jalapeño, cumin, cilantro and avocado give it its south-of-

½ lb. ground mild pork sausage
½ lb. ground beef
1 jalapeño pepper, seeded and finely
   chopped
⅔ c. canned diced tomatoes and
   green chiles
1 t. garlic powder
1 t. ground cumin
½ t. salt
½ t. pepper
10¾-oz. can cream of celery soup

10¾-oz. can cream of mushro
   soup
10-oz. can enchilada sauce
18 (6-inch) corn tortillas
2 c. shredded Cheddar cheese
1 c. shredded Monterey Jack
   cheese
1 tomato, seeded and diced
4 green onions, chopped
¼ c. fresh cilantro, chopped
Optional: 1 avocado, chopped

Cook sausage and ground beef in a large skillet over medium-high heat,
stirring until meat crumbles and is no longer pink. Drain. Stir in jalapeño and
next 5 ingredients; cook until thoroughly heated.

Stir together soups and enchilada sauce in a saucepan; cook until thoroughly heated.

Spoon one-third of sauce onto bottom of a lightly greased 13"x9" baking
dish; top with 6 tortillas. Spoon half of beef mixture and one-third of sauce
over tortillas; sprinkle with half of Cheddar cheese. Top with 6 tortillas;
repeat layers, ending with tortillas. Sprinkle with Monterey Jack cheese and
next 3 ingredients.

Bake at 350 degrees for 30 minutes. Top with avocado, if desired. Serves
6 to 8.

beef in rosemary-mushroom sauce
(pictured on page 46)

Add some roasted redskin potatoes and a simple tossed salad for an oh-so-elegant yet easy dinner!

1-lb. boneless top sirloin steak, about ¾-inch thick
8-oz. pkg. sliced mushrooms
1 c. white wine or chicken broth
10½-oz. can beef broth
8-oz. can tomato sauce

1 c. green onions, chopped
¼ c. fresh parsley, chopped and divided
1½ t. fresh rosemary, chopped
1½ t. balsamic vinegar
4 cloves garlic, minced

Place steak in a large plastic zipping bag; top with mushrooms and wine or broth. Refrigerate 30 minutes, turning occasionally. Remove steak from bag, reserving mushrooms and marinade.

Lightly spray a large non-stick skillet with non-stick vegetable spray and place over medium-high heat. Add steak and cook 6 minutes or to desired degree of doneness, turning after 3 minutes. Remove steak from skillet; keep warm.

Combine beef broth, tomato sauce, green onions, 2 tablespoons parsley and next 3 ingredients in a medium bowl. Add parsley mixture, mushrooms and marinade to skillet; bring to a boil. Cook until reduced to 2 cups, about 15 minutes, stirring frequently. Thinly slice steak diagonally across the grain and place on a serving platter. Spoon sauce over steak; sprinkle with remaining 2 tablespoons parsley. Serves 4.

Sharon Demers
Dolores, CO

green pepper steak

Slicing meat across the grain yields tender results. Place an electric knife or sharp chef's knife at an angle against the grain of the meat.

1-lb. round steak
¼ c. soy sauce
1 clove garlic, diced
1½ t. fresh ginger, peeled and grated
2 T. canola oil
1 c. green onions, thinly sliced

1 c. green pepper, thinly sliced
1 rib celery, thinly sliced
1 T. cornstarch
1 c. water
2 tomatoes, coarsely chopped

Slice steak across the grain into thin strips about ⅛-inch thick. Stir together soy sauce, garlic and ginger in a large bowl; add steak and toss well.

Heat oil in a deep skillet; add steak and cook over medium-high heat 6 minutes or until browned. Cover and simmer 25 minutes over medium heat. Adjust heat to medium-high; add green onions, green pepper and celery. Cook 10 minutes or until vegetables are crisp-tender.

Whisk together cornstarch and water until smooth; add to pan. Stir and cook 4 minutes or until thickened; add tomatoes and heat thoroughly. Serves 4.

Kendall Hale
Lynn, MA

"My husband's favorite after a hard day!"

Kendall

perfect prime rib

This succulent cut of meat doesn't need a lot of help in the flavor department, but a serving of horseradish sauce is always a welcome addition.

¼ c. Worcestershire sauce
2 t. garlic powder
2 t. seasoned salt

2 t. pepper
6-lb. bone-in beef rib roast

Combine all ingredients except roast in a small bowl. Rub mixture over roast; place in a large plastic zipping bag. Refrigerate 8 hours or overnight, turning often.

Place roast, fat-side up, in a lightly greased large roasting pan; pour mixture from bag over roast. Cover with aluminum foil; bake at 350 degrees for 1½ hours. Uncover and bake 1½ more hours or until a meat thermometer inserted into thickest portion registers 145 degrees (medium rare) or to desired degree of doneness. Let stand for 15 minutes before slicing. Serves 6 to 8.

Paula Smith
Ottawa, IL

"For special dinners, this recipe never lets me down!"

Paula

Mom's Sicilian pot roast

Rotini pasta adds to the Sicilian twist of this pot roast...as do the other Italian flavors. It would be just as yummy served over hot cooked rice or savory mashed potatoes.

4-lb. rolled rump beef roast
2 T. garlic-flavored olive oil
2 (28-oz.) cans whole tomatoes
2 (8-oz.) cans Italian tomato sauce
½ c. water
1 T. garlic, minced
1 t. dried oregano
1 t. dried basil

1 t. dried parsley
1½ t. salt
½ t. pepper
Optional: ¼ c. all-purpose flour,
    2 c. hot water
hot cooked rotini pasta
Garnish: fresh oregano sprigs

Brown roast slowly in oil over medium heat in a Dutch oven. Add tomatoes, tomato sauce, water, garlic and seasonings to Dutch oven. Bring to a boil; cover, reduce heat and simmer 2½ hours or until tender, turning occasionally.

Cut roast into serving-size slices. Return meat to Dutch oven; simmer, uncovered, 30 more minutes. If sauce is not thick enough, combine flour and water, stirring until dissolved. Gradually stir flour mixture into sauce, a little at a time, until sauce thickens. To serve, place prepared pasta on a large platter; top with sauce and sliced meat. Garnish with fresh oregano sprigs, if desired. Serves 8 to 10.

Barbara Rannazzisi
Gainesville, VA

"We start this dish early in the morning so it's cooking while appetizers are nibbled on during football games. Serve it with a crisp salad and garlic bread. Life doesn't get any better than this!"

Barbara

pepper-crusted roast beef
(pictured on page 312)

A caramelized-onion sauce is spooned over slices of roast beef.

2- to 3-lb. boneless beef rib roast
¼ c. garlic, minced
½ t. salt
3 T. peppercorns
¼ c. Worcestershire sauce

2 red onions, thinly sliced
1 T. canola oil
1 T. brown sugar, packed
2 T. balsamic vinegar

Rub roast with garlic and salt; coat fat side of roast with peppercorns. Drizzle with Worcestershire sauce. Place in a roaster pan. Bake at 350 degrees for 2 hours and 15 minutes or until a meat thermometer inserted into thickest portion registers 145 degrees (medium rare) or 160 degrees (medium). Shield with aluminum foil during cooking if roast gets too brown.

Cook onions in oil in a large skillet over medium heat until onions are soft. Add brown sugar and vinegar; cook about 8 to 10 minutes or until onions are caramelized. Let stand 10 minutes; slice roast and serve onions over top. Serves 6 to 8.

Linda Behling
Cecil, PA

garnish, if desired

Use simple garnishes to dress up main dishes throughout the year. Fresh mint sprigs add coolness and color to summertime dishes, while rosemary sprigs and cranberries arranged to resemble holly add a festive touch to holiday platters.

marinated brisket

The long cook time guarantees tender slices of this lean cut of meat.

¼ c. soy sauce
1 T. celery salt
2 T. smoke-flavored cooking sauce
1 T. Worcestershire sauce
2 t. onion salt
2 t. garlic salt
2 t. salt
2 t. pepper

4- to 5-lb. beef brisket, trimmed
½ c. catsup
3 T. brown sugar, packed
1 T. soy sauce
1 t. dry mustard
1 t. lemon juice
3 drops hot sauce
⅛ t. nutmeg

Stir together first 8 ingredients in a small bowl. Pour over brisket and marinate overnight in the refrigerator, turning every few hours.

Remove from marinade. Bake at 350 degrees for 3½ hours. Stir together catsup and next 6 ingredients and pour over brisket during the last 45 minutes of cooking time. Serves 8.

Neta Jo Liebscher
El Reno, OK

"I like to put my brisket on early Sunday morning so that it will be ready for a houseful after church. Growing up, my children were spoiled with homegrown beef, and brisket was their favorite. Now that they're grown, my husband and I look forward to the Sundays when they and their families come home for their favorite Mom-cooked meal."

Neta Jo

Simple Sloppy Joes,
page 125

fast family suppers

Getting supper to the table fast is a priority for families on-the-go, and most of these recipes can be ready in 30 minutes or less. Try breakfast for dinner one night and serve up hearty Country-Style Supper Skillet (page 92). Don't forget comforting favorites like Momma's Divine Divan (page 109) or Cheesy Tuna Tempter (page 104). Bring the family back to the table with these quick & easy choices.

country-style supper skillet
(pictured on page 313)

Eggs, fresh tomatoes, bacon and potatoes make up this hearty dish you'll serve again and again.

½ lb. bacon, chopped
3 c. potatoes, peeled, cooked and
   diced
1 c. tomato, chopped
½ c. onion, chopped
½ c. green pepper, chopped

1 t. garlic, chopped
½ t. salt
¼ t. pepper
1½ c. shredded sharp Cheddar
   cheese
8 eggs

Cook bacon over medium heat in a large deep skillet until crisp; partially drain drippings, reserving some in skillet.

Add vegetables, garlic, salt and pepper; sauté in pan drippings about 5 minutes or until tender. Sprinkle with cheese. Make 8 wells for eggs; crack eggs into wells about 2 inches apart. Reduce heat; cover and cook eggs over medium heat 10 to 12 minutes or to desired degree of doneness. Serves 4 to 6.

Rita Morgan
Pueblo, CO

ham, mushroom & bacon quiche

Your entire family will love this quiche…it's loaded with cheese, bacon and ham.

6 eggs, beaten
¾ c. milk
salt and pepper to taste
1 c. shredded Cheddar cheese
2 to 3 slices bacon, crisply cooked
   and crumbled

4 slices deli ham, chopped
4-oz. can sliced mushrooms,
   drained
9-inch unbaked pie crust

Mix together eggs and milk in a medium bowl. Add salt and pepper; set aside.

Sprinkle cheese, bacon, ham and mushrooms on top of pie crust; pour egg mixture over top. Bake at 350 degrees for 25 to 30 minutes or until a toothpick inserted in center comes out clean and top is golden. Serves 4.

Kaitlyn Kiser
Plainwell, MI

"I've made this substituting spinach and sausage or potatoes and broccoli for the ham, mushrooms and bacon. It's fun to experiment with lots of different ingredient combinations!"

Kaitlyn

simply scrumptious frittata

Just cook cubed redskin potatoes in 2 tablespoons of oil in a large skillet until tender and golden before adding them to this hearty frittata.

1 T. vegetable oil
½ c. onion, chopped
½ c. green pepper, chopped
1 to 2 cloves garlic, minced
4 redskin potatoes, peeled,
    cubed and cooked

¾ c. cubed cooked ham
8 eggs, beaten
½ t. salt
pepper to taste
¾ c. shredded Cheddar cheese

Heat oil in a heavy oven-proof non-stick 10" skillet over medium heat. Add onion and green pepper; cook and stir until tender. Add garlic; cook one more minute. Stir in potatoes and ham; cook until thoroughly heated.

Reduce heat to medium-low; add eggs, salt and pepper. Cook about 5 minutes or until eggs are firm on the bottom. Top with cheese; place in oven and bake at 350 degrees for 5 to 10 minutes or until cheese melts. Cut into wedges. Serves 4.

Jill Valentine
Jackson, TN

"A tasty way to use any remaining ham from Sunday dinner...try different cheeses for variety."

Jill

lucky-7 mac & cheese

Seven varieties of cheese come together in this favorite homestyle dish that stirs up quickly on the cooktop rather than baking in the oven. We consider whoever gets a serving of this...lucky!

1 c. fat-free milk
½ c. extra sharp Cheddar
   cheese, cubed
½ c. Colby cheese, cubed
½ c. pasteurized process
   cheese spread, cubed
½ c. Swiss cheese, cubed

½ c. provolone cheese, cubed
½ c. Monterey Jack cheese, cubed
½ c. crumbled blue cheese
16-oz. pkg. elbow macaroni,
   cooked
salt and pepper to taste

Cook milk and cheeses in a heavy 4-quart saucepan over low heat until cheeses melt, whisking often. Stir in macaroni; season with salt and pepper. Heat thoroughly. Serves 6 to 8.

Tina Vogel
Orlando, FL

Greek pizza

Mediterranean ingredients like olives, capers, fresh basil and feta cheese make up the flavorful toppings of this Greek-inspired pizza.

13.8-oz. tube refrigerated pizza
   dough
olive oil
2 cloves garlic, minced
8-oz. pkg. shredded mozzarella
   cheese, divided
½ c. canned artichokes, drained
   and chopped

¼ c. sliced green olives
½ c. fresh basil, thinly sliced
¼ c. crumbled feta cheese
3 T. capers
Optional: 6 anchovy fillets, finely
   chopped

"Don't let the anchovies keep you from trying this...they're completely optional!"

Sean

Roll out pizza dough on a floured surface to about ¼-inch thick. Place on a lightly greased baking sheet; brush lightly with olive oil.

Spread garlic over dough; sprinkle with half of mozzarella. Top with artichokes, olives, basil, feta, capers and, if desired, anchovies. Sprinkle with remaining half of mozzarella. Bake at 400 degrees for 8 to 10 minutes or until cheese melts. Serves 4.

Sean Avner
Delaware, OH

pizza party

Almost everyone loves pizza, so why not provide the crust and sauce, then invite friends to visit and share their favorite toppings? You might create a new combination!

vegetable lo mein à la Rob

Lo mein noodles are usually the key ingredient in this Asian dish, but the "à la Rob" version of this dish substitutes rice noodles. We'll let you choose...it's good either way.

8-oz. pkg. rice noodles, cooked
2 T. plus 1 t. sesame oil, divided
½ t. salt
1 onion, halved and sliced into
    crescents
2 ribs celery, thinly sliced
2 cloves garlic, pressed
1½ t. fresh ginger, peeled and
    shredded

1 carrot, peeled and shredded
¼ lb. snow peas
1 c. sliced mushrooms
1 c. frozen corn kernels
Optional: dry white wine or
    vegetable broth
Sauce

Toss noodles in a bowl with one teaspoon sesame oil and salt; set aside.

Heat remaining 2 tablespoons oil in a skillet over high heat. Add onion and next 7 ingredients, one at a time, in order given; stir-fry each 2 to 4 minutes until crisp-tender. Add a little white wine or vegetable broth to skillet if skillet gets too dry. Pour noodles on top and reduce heat to low. Drizzle Sauce over noodles and toss together. Serves 4 to 6.

sauce:

½ c. dry white wine or vegetable
    broth
¼ c. sugar
1½ T. cornstarch
6 T. soy sauce

4 t. hoisin sauce
2 t. sesame oil
1 t. rice wine vinegar or white
    vinegar

Combine all ingredients in a small saucepan. Cook over low heat 5 minutes or until thickened. Keep warm. Makes one cup.

Robbin Chamberlain
Worthington, OH

"A savory main dish that's much easier than it looks...chop the veggies and stir up the sauce, and it goes together very quickly."

Robbin

fresh tomato & basil linguine

If ripe garden tomatoes are out of season, chopped roma tomatoes or halved cherry tomatoes are good substitutes.

1½ lbs. tomatoes, finely chopped
3 cloves garlic, minced
1 red pepper, chopped
1 bunch fresh basil, torn
½ c. olive oil

1 t. salt
pepper to taste
16-oz. pkg. linguine, cooked
Garnish: grated Parmesan cheese

Stir together tomatoes, garlic, red pepper and basil in a large bowl; drizzle with oil. Sprinkle with salt and pepper; mix well and toss with hot cooked linguine. Sprinkle with Parmesan cheese, if desired. Serves 6 to 8.

Vickie
Gooseberry Patch

lemon-pepper fish

Feel free to substitute either pollock or haddock for the cod in this recipe. Each option is a white fish and a member of the cod family.

1 lb. frozen cod, thawed
16-oz. pkg. frozen stir-fry vegetables
salt to taste
1 t. lemon-pepper seasoning

1 t. dried rosemary
1 c. tomato juice
2½ T. grated Parmesan cheese

Line a 13"x9" baking dish with aluminum foil. Place cod on foil and cover with vegetables. Season with salt, lemon-pepper seasoning and rosemary. Pour tomato juice over ingredients in dish; sprinkle with Parmesan cheese. Bake at 400 degrees for 20 to 25 minutes or until fish flakes easily with a fork and vegetables are tender. Serves 4.

Liz Plotnick-Snay
Gooseberry Patch

"A scrumptious, light dinner."

Liz

al fresco dining

Dinners at home don't have to be in the kitchen…and the outdoors isn't reserved for cookouts. Bake up a tasty dish inside, then lead everyone to the backyard…they'll be so surprised!

fettuccine with smoked salmon

Fresh asparagus and dill pair up with creamy fettuccine and smoked salmon for a refreshing springtime meal.

8-oz. pkg. fettuccine, uncooked
1 lb. asparagus, cut into ½-inch
    pieces
1 c. whipping cream
2 T. fresh dill, chopped
1 T. prepared horseradish

4 oz. smoked salmon, cut into
    ½-inch pieces
½ t. salt
¼ t. pepper
freshly squeezed lemon juice

Cook pasta according to package directions; add asparagus during last 3 minutes of cooking time. Drain and set aside.

Heat cream, dill and horseradish in a skillet over low heat about one minute or until hot; add pasta mixture, tossing to mix. Gently toss in salmon; add salt and pepper. Squeeze lemon juice over top. Serves 4 to 6.

Carole Larkins
Elmendorf AFB, AK

"I like to serve this spooned into a serving bowl ringed with fresh lettuce leaves."

Carole

cheesy tuna tempter

Tuna casserole is the ultimate comfort food. This version is made even more comfy with the addition of 2 types of cheeses.

½ c. celery, chopped
¼ c. onion, chopped
5 T. butter, divided
10¾-oz. can cream of mushroom soup
1½ c. milk, divided
6-oz. can tuna, drained
1 c. finely shredded sharp Cheddar cheese
½ c. grated Parmesan cheese
¼ t. salt
¼ t. pepper
8-oz. pkg. medium egg noodles, cooked
10 round buttery crackers, crushed

Sauté celery and onion in 2 tablespoons butter in a large skillet over medium heat until tender. Add soup, milk, tuna, cheeses, salt and pepper; mix well.

Place noodles in a lightly greased 2-quart baking dish. Pour tuna mixture over top; toss to coat noodles. Sprinkle cracker crumbs on top and dot with remaining 3 tablespoons butter. Bake at 350 degrees for 25 minutes or until hot and bubbly. Serves 4 to 6.

Charity Meyer
Lewisberry, PA

shrimply divine casserole

Don't wait for special occasions to serve shrimp. This dish is easy enough to whip up during the week...your family will thank you for it!

8-oz. pkg. spinach egg noodles, cooked
3-oz. pkg. cream cheese, cubed
1½ lbs. uncooked medium shrimp, peeled and cleaned
½ c. butter
10¾-oz. can cream of mushroom soup

1 c. sour cream
½ c. milk
½ c. mayonnaise
1 T. fresh chives, chopped
½ t. mustard
Optional: ¾ c. shredded cheese

Place noodles in a lightly greased 13"x9" baking dish. Place cream cheese cubes on hot noodles; set aside.

Sauté shrimp in butter in a large skillet over medium heat until shrimp turn pink; place over noodles and cheese.

Stir together soup and next 5 ingredients; pour over shrimp. Sprinkle shredded cheese on top, if desired. Bake at 325 degrees for 20 to 30 minutes or until bubbly. Serves 6.

Karen Puchnick
Butler, PA

Thai peanut noodles

If you want to purchase raw shrimp and cook and peel it yourself, start with 2 pounds. Chicken breasts are a nice substitute for shrimp in this peanutty-flavored Asian dish. For 4 servings, use 4 boneless breasts. Cut the chicken into bite-size chunks and sauté in a little oil ahead of time.

1 lb. cooked, peeled medium shrimp
1 c. light Italian salad dressing, divided
2 T. crunchy peanut butter
1 T. soy sauce
1 T. honey
1 t. ground ginger

¾ t. red pepper flakes
1 carrot, peeled and shredded
1 c. green onions, chopped
1 T. sesame oil
8-oz. pkg. angel hair pasta, cooked
2 T. fresh cilantro, chopped
Optional: ⅔ c. peanuts, chopped

Coat shrimp with ½ cup Italian salad dressing; refrigerate 30 minutes.

Whisk together remaining ½ cup Italian salad dressing, peanut butter, soy sauce, honey, ginger and red pepper flakes until smooth; set aside.

Sauté carrot, green onions and shrimp in sesame oil about 5 minutes or until shrimp are thoroughly heated. Toss pasta, peanut sauce and shrimp mixture together in a large serving bowl; sprinkle with cilantro and, if desired, peanuts. Serves 4.

Emily Selmer
Sumner, WA

chicken burritos
(pictured on page 309)

These burritos are the perfect solution for what to serve on those busy nights when you need supper in a hurry! Just add Mexican rice or black beans to go along.

4 boneless, skinless chicken
   breasts, cooked and shredded
1½ c. salsa, divided
1 c. sour cream
6 (10-inch) flour tortillas

10¾-oz. can cream of chicken soup
2 c. shredded Mexican-blend cheese
Toppings: chopped tomatoes, sliced
   green onions, sour cream

Combine chicken, ½ cup salsa and sour cream in a large bowl. Spoon chicken mixture evenly onto tortillas. Fold up sides and roll up, burrito-style; place in an ungreased 13"x9" baking dish. Blend together soup and remaining one cup salsa; pour over burritos.

Bake, uncovered, at 350 degrees for 30 minutes. Sprinkle with cheese and bake 5 more minutes or until cheese melts. Serve with desired toppings. Serves 6.

Karen Wright
Arnold, MO

Momma's divine divan

(pictured on page 306)

Choose rotisserie chicken from your supermarket deli to add more flavor to this family favorite. Generally, one rotisserie chicken will yield 3 cups of chopped meat, so you'll need 2 rotisserie chickens to get the 4 to 5 cups needed for this recipe. Add cooked rice, and you have a complete meal!

½ lb. broccoli flowerets, cooked

4 to 5 boneless, skinless chicken
   breasts, cooked and cubed

salt to taste

1 c. seasoned bread crumbs

1 T. butter, melted

10¾-oz. can cream of chicken soup

½ c. mayonnaise

1 t. curry powder

½ t. lemon juice

1 c. shredded Cheddar cheese

Arrange broccoli in the bottom of a lightly greased 13"x9" baking dish. Sprinkle chicken with salt to taste; place on top of broccoli and set aside.

Toss together bread crumbs and butter; set aside.

Combine soup, mayonnaise, curry powder and lemon juice in a small bowl; spread over chicken and broccoli. Top with cheese; sprinkle with bread crumb mixture. Bake, uncovered, at 350 degrees for 25 minutes. Serves 8 to 10.

Margaret Vinci
Pasadena, CA

savory substitute

Fresh out of bread crumbs for this crunchy topping? Use herb-flavored stuffing mix instead, and the casserole will be just as yummy!

chicken chimies

Add a bit of heat to this Mexican favorite by using pepper Jack cheese in place of regular Monterey Jack.

2 boneless, skinless chicken breasts,
    cooked and shredded
salt, pepper and garlic salt to taste
1 T. butter
10 (8-inch) flour tortillas
8-oz. pkg. shredded Monterey Jack
    cheese

6 green onions, diced
1 T. vegetable oil
Toppings: sour cream, guacamole,
    salsa
Optional: lettuce leaves

Sprinkle chicken with salt, pepper and garlic salt to taste. Heat butter in a large skillet over medium heat; add chicken and sauté about 3 minutes.

Spoon chicken evenly onto tortillas. Top with cheese and green onions; fold up sides and roll up, burrito-style. Heat oil in a large skillet over medium-high heat. Add rolled-up tortillas and sauté until golden. Serve with your choice of toppings and over lettuce leaves, if desired. Serves 6 to 8.

Diana Duff
Cypress, CA

> "Why go out to eat when this is just as good as any restaurant?"
>
> **Diana**

clever condiments!

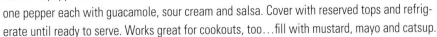

When serving a Mexican meal with a trio of toppings, such as these chimichangas, slice the tops off 3 bell peppers, rinse and remove seeds. Then fill one pepper each with guacamole, sour cream and salsa. Cover with reserved tops and refrigerate until ready to serve. Works great for cookouts, too…fill with mustard, mayo and catsup.

gobbler cobbler

There's no such thing as boring leftovers when you serve dishes like this!

3 c. cooked turkey, cubed
2½ c. turkey gravy
1½ c. frozen peas, partially thawed
1½ c. sliced mushrooms
⅔ c. sun-dried tomatoes, chopped
¼ c. water

2 T. fresh parsley, chopped and
    divided
1 t. poultry seasoning, divided
2¼ c. buttermilk biscuit baking mix
¼ t. pepper
¾ c. plus 2 T. milk

Combine turkey, gravy, peas, mushrooms, tomatoes, water, one tablespoon parsley and ½ teaspoon poultry seasoning in a large stockpot. Cook over medium heat until mixture comes to a boil, stirring occasionally.

Stir together baking mix, remaining one tablespoon parsley, remaining ½ teaspoon poultry seasoning, pepper and milk in another bowl. Pour turkey mixture into a lightly greased 2-quart baking dish; drop biscuit mixture on top in 6 equal mounds. Place dish on a baking sheet; bake at 450 degrees for 20 minutes or until topping is golden. Serves 6.

Sandy Rowe
Bellevue, OH

casserole topper

Create a topper for your favorite casserole. Unroll 2 refrigerated pie crusts; sprinkle one with pecans and sun-dried tomatoes (or any other goodies) and top with remaining crust. Roll crusts together and cut into shapes with cookie cutters. Bake at 425 degrees for 8 minutes and arrange on the baked casserole before serving.

maple-cranberry turkey

For a small holiday gathering, this recipe is just the ticket. Turkey breast tenderloins yield enough for 4 servings. Cranberries, cinnamon and sweet potatoes give you all the flavors of the season.

1-lb. pkg. turkey breast tenderloins
1 T. olive oil
⅓ c. sweetened dried cranberries
⅓ c. maple syrup
¼ c. orange juice
1 T. butter
¼ t. cinnamon
29-oz. can cut sweet potatoes

Brown turkey in oil in an 11" skillet over medium heat 6 to 7 minutes on each side; set aside.

Bring cranberries, syrup, orange juice, butter and cinnamon to a boil in a saucepan; remove from heat. Add sweet potatoes to turkey in skillet; pour cranberry mixture on top.

Cook over medium heat 30 minutes or until turkey is done and sauce thickens. Serves 4.

Delinda Blakney
Bridgeview, IL

"Just right for chilly autumn evenings."

Delinda

Santa Fe pork cutlets

Salsa, corn and cilantro give this tenderloin its Santa Fe flair. Let your taste buds be the judge regarding whether you go for mild or spicy salsa.

3 T. all-purpose flour
¼ t. salt
⅛ t. pepper
1-lb. pork tenderloin, sliced ¼-inch
    thick
3 t. vegetable oil, divided

½ c. salsa
½ c. thawed frozen corn kernels
¼ c. water
Toppings: sour cream, chopped
    fresh cilantro

Combine flour, salt and pepper; dredge pork in flour mixture. Heat 2 teaspoons oil over medium heat in a non-stick skillet. Sauté half the cutlets one to 1½ minutes per side. Transfer to a plate. Repeat with remaining one teaspoon oil and cutlets. Cover to keep warm.

Add salsa, corn and water to skillet. Simmer over medium heat one minute. Remove from heat. Spoon salsa mixture over cutlets. Top with sour cream and chopped cilantro, if desired. Serves 4.

Beverly Ray
Brandon, FL

"What a delicious way to serve pork, and it's so fast!"

Beverly

lemony pork piccata

(pictured on page 307)

Serve over quick-cooking angel hair pasta to enjoy every drop of the lemony sauce.

1-lb. pork tenderloin, sliced into
   8 portions
2 t. lemon-pepper seasoning
3 T. all-purpose flour
2 T. butter

¼ c. dry sherry or chicken broth
¼ c. lemon juice
¼ c. capers
4 to 6 thin slices lemon

Pound pork slices to ⅛-inch thickness, using a meat mallet or rolling pin. Lightly sprinkle pork with lemon-pepper seasoning and flour. Melt one tablespoon butter in a large skillet over medium-high heat. Add half of pork and sauté 2 to 3 minutes on each side until golden, turning once. Repeat procedure with remaining butter and pork. Remove pork to a serving plate; set aside.

Add sherry or chicken broth, lemon juice, capers and lemon slices to skillet. Cook 2 minutes or until slightly thickened, scraping up browned bits. Add pork and heat thoroughly. Serves 4.

Melody Taynor
Everett, WA

honey-pecan pork cutlets

A touch of honey in the pecan sauce adds a hint of sweetness to these pork cutlets.

1 lb. boneless pork loin cutlets
½ c. all-purpose flour
3 T. butter, divided

¼ c. chopped pecans
¼ c. honey

Pound pork to ¼-inch thickness, using a meat mallet or rolling pin. Coat cutlets with flour.

Heat one tablespoon butter in a large skillet over medium heat. Add pork and sauté about 5 to 6 minutes or until brown on both sides.

Soften remaining 2 tablespoons butter in a small mixing bowl and combine with pecans and honey; add to skillet, stirring gently. Cover and simmer 7 to 8 minutes or until done. Remove to a serving platter and spoon sauce over pork. Serves 2 to 3.

Kathy Grashoff
Fort Wayne, IN

"You won't believe that something so good could be so simple."

Kathy

quick table setting

You don't have to spend a lot of time setting the table for casual gatherings. Just wrap colorful napkins around silverware and slip one bundle into a glass at each place setting. It's so charming…and you don't have to remember where the forks, knives and spoons go!

hearty red beans & rice

In New Orleans, beans go hand in hand with rice. It's the official Monday meal there as well. But no matter which day you choose to serve this version of the classic dish, family & friends will leave the table happy.

1 green pepper, chopped
1 onion, chopped
½ c. green onions, chopped
½ c. celery, chopped
2 T. fresh parsley, chopped
3 slices bacon, crisply cooked and
   crumbled, drippings reserved
½ lb. Polish sausage, sliced
2 (15-oz.) cans kidney beans,
   drained and rinsed

1 c. chicken broth
6-oz. can tomato paste
2-oz. jar chopped pimentos, drained
2 T. catsup
1 t. chili powder
1½ t. Worcestershire sauce
3 c. cooked rice

Sauté green pepper, onions, celery and parsley in reserved bacon drippings in a skillet over medium heat until tender.

Stir in bacon, sausage and next 7 ingredients. Reduce heat; cover and simmer 30 minutes, stirring occasionally. Serve over cooked rice. Serves 4.

Kerry Mayer
Denham Springs, LA

"A big bowl of this down-home favorite really hits the spot."

Kerry

bacon florentine fettuccine

Creamed spinach gets a makeover in this recipe when it's paired with crispy bacon and fettuccine.

16-oz. pkg. refrigerated fettuccine, uncooked
2 (10-oz.) pkgs. frozen creamed spinach
½ lb. bacon, crisply cooked and chopped
⅛ t. garlic powder
½ c. plus 2 T. grated Parmesan cheese, divided
pepper to taste

Prepare fettuccine according to package directions; drain, reserving ¾ cup of cooking liquid. Return fettuccine and reserved liquid to saucepan.

Microwave spinach according to package directions. Add spinach, bacon and garlic powder to fettuccine in saucepan, stirring to combine. Transfer to a serving dish and stir in ½ cup cheese. Season with pepper and sprinkle with remaining 2 tablespoons cheese. Serves 4.

Barbara Adamson
Oviedo, FL

tangy brown sugar ham

These thick slices of ham steak are brushed with a sweet-hot sauce and grilled for a pleasing smoky taste.

1 c. brown sugar, packed
⅓ c. prepared horseradish
¼ c. lemon juice

4 slices cooked ham, cut 1-inch
    thick (about 1 lb.)

Combine sugar, horseradish and lemon juice in a saucepan; bring to a boil. Brush over ham.

Grill ham over high heat (400 to 500 degrees) 4 to 6 minutes on each side or until thoroughly heated. Serves 4.

Alyce Leitzel
Hegins, PA

beyond the basics

Look past traditional napkins when hosting family & friends. Try using bandanas, colorful dish towels, inexpensive fabrics from the crafts store or, for especially saucy foods, moistened washcloths.

mini meat loaves

This recipe can also be baked in 6 ungreased muffin cups. Spoon mixture evenly into cups and bake at 350 degrees for 35 minutes.

1 lb. ground beef
1 small onion, finely chopped
2 slices bread, cubed

1 egg, beaten
10¾-oz. can vegetable soup,
    undiluted

Combine all ingredients in a large mixing bowl. Shape into 6 oval loaves. Place on an ungreased rimmed baking sheet. Bake at 350 degrees for 20 minutes. Serve with barbecue sauce, chili sauce, salsa or catsup. Serves 6.

Roxanne Bixby
West Franklin, NH

"For extra fun, use large cookie cutters to shape the meat, then simply place the meat on a cookie sheet to bake."

Roxanne

hamburger-noodle bake

This one-dish meal is easy to make ahead of time and refrigerate or freeze for later...just heat it up when hunger hits!

1 lb. ground beef
½ c. onion, chopped
2 (8-oz.) cans tomato sauce
1 T. sugar
¾ t. garlic salt
¼ t. pepper

4 c. cooked medium egg noodles
1 c. cottage cheese
8-oz. pkg. cream cheese, softened
¼ c. sour cream
¼ c. grated Parmesan cheese

Cook ground beef and onion in a skillet over medium-high heat, stirring until beef crumbles and is no longer pink; drain. Stir in tomato sauce, sugar, garlic salt and pepper; heat thoroughly and remove from heat.

Gently combine noodles, cottage cheese, cream cheese and sour cream; spread half of noodle mixture in a lightly greased 11"x7" baking dish. Layer with half of meat mixture; repeat both layers. Sprinkle with Parmesan cheese; bake at 350 degrees for 30 minutes. Serves 8.

Kate Conroy
Bethlehem, PA

simple sloppy Joes
(pictured on page 90)

These sandwiches will be a winner with the family for their flavor and with Mom for their ease!

1 lb. ground chuck	2 T. Worcestershire sauce
1 onion, chopped	¼ t. salt
1 c. catsup	¼ t. pepper
¼ c. water	6 to 8 sandwich buns

Cook ground chuck and onion in a large skillet over medium-high heat, stirring until beef crumbles and is no longer pink; drain. Stir in catsup, water, Worcestershire sauce, salt and pepper; simmer 20 minutes, stirring frequently. Spoon onto buns. Serves 6 to 8.

Jennifer Catterino
Pasadena, MD

"Just as quick as using canned sauce!"

Jennifer

love of cooking

After graduating from college, I found that I could only "cook" frozen pizza. My idea of a gourmet meal was when I opened up a jar of spaghetti sauce and poured it over pasta. When I got my first job out of school, I met my dear friend, Barbara. Barb would often invite me over for dinner because she loved to cook. I was impressed with her cooking and thought I would give it a try and invite her over for dinner. Well, it didn't work out as I'd hoped. I burned dinner, so we ordered out! That was the beginning of many cooking lessons and wonderful recipes Barb shared with me.

Barb instilled in me a love of cooking and I have no one else to thank but her. She's still the best cook, even though I continue to bake a frozen pizza now and then!

Gina Bass-Yurevich
Springfield, IL

nacho grande casserole

Turn this chunky casserole into a hearty appetizer by providing tortilla chips for dipping.

2 lbs. ground beef
1 onion, chopped
2 (16-oz.) cans spicy chili beans
16-oz. pkg. frozen corn kernels,
    thawed
15-oz. can tomato sauce
1¼-oz. pkg. taco seasoning mix

3 c. finely shredded Cheddar
    Jack cheese, divided
3 c. nacho cheese tortilla
    chips, crushed and divided
Toppings: chopped tomatoes and
    green onions

Cook ground beef and onion in a Dutch oven over medium-high heat, stirring until beef crumbles and is no longer pink; drain. Add beans, corn, tomato sauce and seasoning mix; stir until blended. Simmer over medium heat 10 minutes.

Pour half of beef mixture into a lightly greased 13"x9" baking dish. Top with 1½ cups each of cheese and crushed chips; top with remaining beef mixture and remaining 1½ cups each of cheese and chips. Bake at 350 degrees for 25 to 30 minutes or until bubbly and golden. Sprinkle with chopped tomatoes and green onions, if desired. Serves 8 to 10.

Carol Hickman
Kingsport, TN

spaghetti pie

Spaghetti and pie are top choices of kids and adults alike. This version is a fun way to serve the recipe...in a pie plate, cut into wedges!

8-oz. pkg. spaghetti, cooked
4 eggs, beaten and divided
⅔ c. grated Parmesan cheese
2 c. cottage cheese, drained
1 lb. ground beef

1 c. green pepper, chopped
1 c. onion, chopped
1½ c. spaghetti sauce
1 c. shredded mozzarella cheese

Combine spaghetti with half of beaten eggs and Parmesan cheese; spread in a lightly greased 9" pie plate. Combine cottage cheese and remaining eggs; spread over spaghetti.

Cook ground beef, green pepper and onion in a large skillet over medium-high heat, stirring until beef crumbles and is no longer pink; drain. Stir sauce into beef mixture; spread over cottage cheese mixture.

Bake at 350 degrees for 30 minutes. Top with mozzarella cheese and bake 5 more minutes or until cheese melts. Cut into wedges to serve. Serves 4 to 6.

Susann Kropp
Cairo, NY

skillet enchiladas

These tortillas are stuffed with cheese and olives, then served with a loaded sauce of ground beef and green chiles...yum!

¼ c. vegetable oil
8 (8-inch) corn tortillas
3 c. shredded Cheddar cheese,
   divided

½ c. chopped olives
Enchilada Sauce

Heat oil in a 10" skillet over medium heat; add one tortilla, heating until just softened. Remove to a paper towel; pat dry. Repeat with remaining tortillas.

Fill tortillas evenly with 2½ cups cheese and olives; roll up and place seam-side down in skillet. Pour Enchilada Sauce over tortillas; cook, covered, over medium heat 5 minutes. Sprinkle with remaining ½ cup cheese; cook, uncovered, until cheese melts. Serves 4 to 8.

enchilada sauce:

1 lb. ground beef
½ c. onion, chopped
10¾-oz. can cream of mushroom
   soup

10-oz. can enchilada sauce
⅓ c. milk
2 T. chopped green chiles

Cook ground beef and onion in a large skillet over medium-high heat, stirring until beef crumbles and is no longer pink; drain. Stir in soup and remaining ingredients; simmer 20 to 25 minutes.

Julie Coles
Boise, ID

"Try diced potatoes in place of ground beef for a vegetarian twist."

Julie

Roasted Corn with Rosemary
Butter, page 145

savory sides

Rounding out your meal is a snap with this selection of side dishes. Choose Cuban Black Beans (page 136) to accompany any of the south-of-the-border main dishes. Share the bounty of your garden with savory Tomato Pie (page 163). And when the weather turns cooler, Mom's Red Cabbage (page 144) offers side-dish comfort. With over 25 delectable choices, you can't go wrong!

asparagus with tomato vinaigrette

It's best to remove the woody stem ends of asparagus before cooking. Holding a stalk of asparagus by both ends, bend the cut end until it snaps…it will naturally break where the most tender part begins.

1 lb. fresh asparagus, trimmed
½ t. salt
3 T. olive oil

1½ T. white wine vinegar
½ t. honey
2 large tomatoes, chopped

Add one inch of water to a medium saucepan; bring to a rolling boil. Add asparagus and salt; boil over low heat 3 to 5 minutes or until tender. Drain.

Heat olive oil over low heat in another saucepan; stir in vinegar and honey. Add tomatoes; heat thoroughly. To serve, pour vinaigrette over asparagus. Serves 4 to 6.

broccoli Parmesan
(pictured on page 312)

This recipe calls for just broccoli flowerets, but don't discard the leaves and stalks. Instead, dice or shred them to use in salads and stir-fries.

8 c. broccoli flowerets
2 T. butter
3 T. onion, chopped
2 T. all-purpose flour
1 t. chicken bouillon granules
1¾ c. milk
½ c. shredded Parmesan cheese

½ t. salt
½ t. pepper
½ t. dry mustard
¼ t. ground marjoram
Optional: shredded Parmesan cheese

Steam broccoli, covered, in a steamer basket over boiling water 5 minutes or until crisp-tender. Keep warm.

Meanwhile, melt butter in a heavy saucepan; add onion and sauté until tender. Add flour and bouillon granules, stirring until blended. Cook, stirring constantly, one minute. Gradually add milk; cook over medium heat, stirring constantly, until thickened and bubbly. Stir in ½ cup cheese and next 4 ingredients; pour over broccoli. Sprinkle with additional cheese, if desired. Serves 6 to 8.

candied-glazed baked apples

Red cinnamon candies give these apples a little zip and a lot of color!

¾ c. sugar
⅓ c. red cinnamon candies
1 c. water

4 baking apples
2 t. lemon juice
1 T. butter, diced

Combine sugar, cinnamon candies and water in a saucepan; bring to a boil over high heat, stirring until sugar dissolves. Reduce heat; simmer, uncovered, 2 minutes. Remove from heat; set aside.

Peel top third of each apple. Remove and discard core, leaving bottom intact. Brush top of apples with lemon juice; arrange in a lightly greased 8"x8" baking dish. Dot centers of apples with butter; brush generously with sugar glaze. Bake at 350 degrees, uncovered, for one hour; brush frequently with remaining glaze. Serve warm. Serves 4.

Jackie Smulski
Lyons, IL

Cuban black beans

(pictured on page 309)

These black beans are a perfect accompaniment to either Chicken Burritos (page 108) or Chicken Chimies (page 111). Or add smoked sausage to the beans and serve with Mexican rice for a one-dish meal.

1 onion, chopped
1 small green pepper, chopped
3 cloves garlic, pressed
2 T. olive oil
3 (15-oz.) cans black beans
¼ c. water or chicken broth

1 T. white vinegar
½ t. salt
¼ t. black pepper
Garnishes: chopped green onions,
   chopped tomato, sour cream

Sauté onion, green pepper and garlic in hot oil in a Dutch oven over medium-high heat until tender. Add undrained beans and next 4 ingredients; bring to a boil. Cover, reduce heat and simmer 15 to 20 minutes. To serve, sprinkle beans with chopped green onions and tomato; top with sour cream, if desired. Makes 5½ cups.

dressed-up refried beans

Cook 2 seeded and diced pickled jalapeños, 2 chopped cloves garlic and ¼ cup chopped onion in ¼ cup bacon drippings. Add 2 (16-ounce) cans refried beans; heat thoroughly and stir in ½ teaspoon ground cumin.

green beans amandine
(pictured on page 308)

Amandine is the French term for dishes that are garnished with almonds. Here, slivered almonds are sautéed with minced onion in butter and tossed with fresh green beans.

2 lbs. green beans
1 small ham hock
1 c. water
⅔ c. slivered almonds

⅓ c. onion, minced
3 T. butter, melted
1 t. salt

Wash beans; trim stem ends. Cut beans into 1½-inch pieces. Place in a Dutch oven; add ham hock and water. Bring to a boil; cover, reduce heat and simmer 12 to 15 minutes or until crisp-tender. Drain.

Sauté almonds and onion in butter in Dutch oven until onion is tender. Add beans and salt; toss lightly. Serves 8.

calico beans

This recipe gets its name from the varied colors of the three types of beans that make up this dish.

½ lb. ground beef
1 c. onion, chopped
1 clove garlic, minced
½ lb. bacon, crisply cooked
    and crumbled
3 (16-oz.) cans baked beans in sauce
2 (16-oz.) cans kidney beans,
    drained and rinsed

15¼-oz. can lima beans, drained
    and rinsed
½ c. catsup
¼ c. brown sugar, packed
1 t. salt
1 t. dry mustard
2 t. white vinegar

Cook ground beef, onion and garlic, stirring until beef crumbles and is no longer pink; drain.

Combine ground beef mixture, crumbled bacon, beans and remaining ingredients in a 3-quart baking dish. Bake, covered, at 350 degrees for 45 minutes. Makes 11½ cups.

Cynthia Rogers
Upton, MA

an instant hit!

Core an apple, then scoop out the insides, leaving at least ¼-inch-thick sides...set each on a serving plate and fill with baked beans.

Grannie Hobson's Louisiana red beans

If you don't have enough time to soak the beans overnight, try the quick-soak method: Place beans in a Dutch oven; cover with water 2 inches above beans and bring to a boil. Boil one minute; cover, remove from heat and let stand one hour. Drain and proceed with recipe.

1 lb. dried red kidney beans	1 t. salt
8-oz. ham hock	½ t. black pepper
6 c. water	¼ t. dried oregano
3 c. onion, chopped	¼ t. dried thyme
1 c. green onions, chopped	⅛ t. hot pepper sauce
1 green pepper, chopped	1 T. Worcestershire sauce
½ c. fresh parsley, chopped	1 lb. cooked ham, chopped
2 cloves garlic, minced	2 t. vegetable oil

Place beans in a Dutch oven. Cover with water 2 inches above beans and let soak 8 hours or overnight. Drain beans; rinse thoroughly and drain again.

Place beans and ham hock in a large stockpot. Add 6 cups water to beans; bring to a boil. Add onion and next 10 ingredients; cover, reduce heat and simmer 2 hours and 15 minutes, stirring occasionally.

Meanwhile, cook ham in oil until lightly browned. Stir into beans and cook, uncovered, 30 minutes. Remove ham hock before serving. Makes 11 cups.

Kristi Hobson
Grapeland, TX

roasted cauliflower

Roasting the cauliflower and onion gives these vegetables a slightly charred appearance and a subtle sweetness and mellow flavor…no sauce is needed.

1 T. olive oil
½ t. garlic powder
¼ t. salt
¼ t. freshly ground black pepper

1 head cauliflower, cut into
   flowerets
1 red onion, cut into ½-inch-thick
   wedges

Place a large jelly-roll pan in a 500-degree oven for 5 minutes or until hot. Meanwhile, combine oil and next 3 ingredients in a large bowl. Add cauliflower and onion; stir well until coated. Pour vegetables onto hot jelly-roll pan and spread into a single layer. Bake at 500 degrees for 15 minutes or until browned, stirring occasionally. Serves 4 to 5.

Karen Puchnick
Butler, PA

"This is a tasty substitute for deep-fried cauliflower!"

Karen

orange-maple glazed carrots

Feel free to use ¼ teaspoon of ground nutmeg in place of the freshly grated nutmeg.

⅓ c. orange juice
12 carrots, peeled and thinly sliced
zest of one orange

3 T. maple syrup
2 T. butter
1 t. grated nutmeg

Microwave orange juice in a microwave-safe baking dish on high for 1½ minutes. Add carrots and orange zest; stir to coat. Cover and microwave on high 7 minutes. Stir in syrup, butter and nutmeg; microwave, uncovered, for 2 minutes. Carrots should be crisp-tender; if not, microwave 2 more minutes. Sprinkle with additional nutmeg, if desired. Serves 4.

Elizabeth Blackstone
Racine, WI

"This dish always impresses guests...don't let them know you made it in the microwave."

Elizabeth

Mom's red cabbage
(pictured on page 310)

We used Braeburn apples for their firmness and sweet yet tart flavor. They're a good accompaniment to the red cabbage.

10 slices bacon, diced
1 onion, diced
1 head red cabbage,
    shredded
½ c. sugar
⅓ c. cider vinegar

1 t. chicken bouillon granules
1 bay leaf
1 c. applesauce
1 c. jellied cranberry sauce
2 apples, peeled and sliced

Cook bacon in a large skillet until crisp; reserve 2 tablespoons drippings in skillet. Add onion to drippings in skillet and sauté until tender. Add cabbage, sugar, vinegar, bouillon granules and bay leaf; cook 8 minutes. Add applesauce, cranberry sauce and apples; simmer 10 minutes or until apples are crisp-tender. Remove and discard bay leaf. Makes 7 cups.

Lisa Rubach
Elkhorn, WI

roasted corn with rosemary butter
(pictured on page 130)

The next time you fire up the grill, make room for this corn on the cob. Nothing could be better than fresh sweet corn roasted in the husk. Peak season for corn is May through September, so enjoy its abundance!

6 ears yellow or white sweet corn, in husks

¼ c. butter, softened

1 t. fresh rosemary, chopped

Pull back corn husks, leaving them attached. Remove and discard silks. Combine butter and rosemary in a small bowl; brush over corn. Pull husks over corn and grill corn over medium-high heat (350 to 400 degrees) for about 15 minutes, turning occasionally. Serves 6.

double-duty grilling

Roast vegetables alongside the meat…brush slices of squash, potatoes, bell peppers or eggplant with olive oil and grill until tender. They're delicious warm or cold, so be sure to grill plenty for sides now and salads later.

Grandma Lucy's corn fritters

Showcase the bounty of summer corn with a batch of these delicately fried fritters. When sweet corn is not at its peak, substitute 3 cups of canned or frozen corn kernels.

4 ears sweet corn, cooked
2 eggs, beaten
¼ c. milk
½ c. all-purpose flour
1 t. baking powder

1 t. sugar
½ t. salt
1 T. bacon drippings or vegetable oil
Optional: butter and maple syrup

Cut kernels from corn and place in a medium mixing bowl; stir in eggs and milk. Combine flour, baking powder, sugar and salt in a small bowl; stir into corn mixture, and mix gently.

Heat bacon drippings or vegetable oil in a skillet over medium-high heat. Drop batter by ¼ cupfuls and cook until delicately browned, turning to brown the other side. Serve with butter and maple syrup, if desired. Makes one dozen.

Carole Griffin
Mount Vernon, OH

"These fritters remind me of my childhood and the golden days of summer when my grandmother made them."

Carole

cracked pepper linguine
(pictured on page 307)

This creamy dish is versatile enough to pair with most entrées. See the spring menu on page 307 where it accompanies Lemony Pork Piccata.

8-oz. pkg. linguine, uncooked
1 T. butter
¼ c. onion, minced
2 cloves garlic, pressed
8-oz. container sour cream
1 T. milk

½ t. salt
2 to 3 t. cracked black pepper
2 T. grated Parmesan cheese
2 T. fresh parsley, chopped
Garnish: fresh parsley sprigs

Cook pasta according to package directions.

Melt butter in a small skillet over medium-high heat. Add onion and garlic and sauté until crisp-tender. Remove mixture from heat and cool slightly.

Stir in sour cream, milk, salt and pepper. Toss with pasta. Sprinkle with cheese and parsley. Garnish, if desired. Serves 4.

Vidalia onion pie with mushrooms

A Vidalia onion is a sweet onion, not a hot one. And not every sweet onion can be called a Vidalia…only those grown within a designated area around Vidalia, Georgia.

1 large Vidalia onion, halved and
    thinly sliced
2 c. shiitake mushrooms, sliced
1 T. olive oil
4 eggs, beaten
1 c. whipping cream

1 T. fresh thyme, chopped
1½ t. salt
1 t. pepper
⅛ t. ground nutmeg
9-inch frozen deep-dish pie crust,
    thawed

Sauté onion and mushrooms in hot oil in a large skillet over medium heat 15 minutes or until tender.

Stir together eggs and next 5 ingredients in a large bowl; stir in onion mixture. Spoon mixture into pie crust and place on a baking sheet.

Bake on lower oven rack at 350 degrees for 45 minutes or until done. Serves 4 to 6.

Note: Feel free to substitute any type of mushroom for the shiitakes.

veggie market

Take the kids along to a farmers' market. Let each choose a vegetable and help prepare it…even picky eaters will want to eat their very own prepared dish.

loaded mashed potato casserole

These mashed potatoes are full of great flavor. They'll definitely be a hands-down winner with the hungry crew who gets invited over to try them.

5½ c. mashed potatoes
½ c. milk
8-oz. pkg. cream cheese, softened
8-oz. container sour cream
2 t. dried parsley

1 t. garlic salt
¼ t. ground nutmeg
¾ c. shredded Cheddar cheese
6 slices bacon, crisply cooked and
   crumbled

Combine all ingredients except Cheddar cheese and bacon in a large mixing bowl. Beat at medium-high speed with an electric mixer until smooth. Spoon into a lightly greased 13"x9" baking dish; top with Cheddar cheese and bacon. Cover and bake at 350 degrees for 30 minutes. Uncover and bake 10 more minutes or until cheese melts. Serves 12.

Tami Bowman
Gooseberry Patch

"When you're in a pinch for time, speed up the prep for this casserole by using prepackaged mashed potatoes and precooked bacon."

Tami

crispy potato pancakes

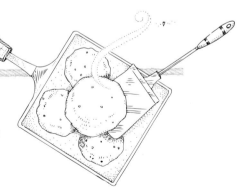

Making these pancakes is a great way to use up extra mashed potatoes. Stir an egg yolk and some minced onion into 2 cups of potatoes. Form into patties and fry in butter until golden. They're delicious served with grilled sausage.

creamed peas
(pictured on page 310)

Salmon and fresh peas are a traditional New England Independence Day dish. We also like the peas paired with Maple-Curry Pork Roast from our fall menu on page 310.

1 T. butter
1 T. vegetable oil
1 c. onion, finely chopped

4 c. frozen baby sweet peas, thawed
½ c. whipping cream
salt and pepper to taste

Melt butter with oil in a large saucepan over low heat. Add onion and cook, stirring frequently, about 11 minutes or until tender and golden. Add peas and cook about 15 minutes or until peas are very tender. Add cream and cook about 5 or 6 minutes until the liquid thickens into a sauce. Season with salt and pepper to taste. Serves 6 to 8.

rosemary potatoes

If you have access to fresh rosemary, substitute an equal amount for the dried.

4 to 6 redskin potatoes,
   peeled and quartered
¼ c. olive oil
2 T. lemon juice

2 cloves garlic, minced
1 to 2 t. dried rosemary, crushed
salt and pepper to taste

Toss together all ingredients in a large bowl; spoon into a greased 13"x9" baking pan. Bake at 350 degrees for one hour. Serves 4 to 6.

Gayle Burns
Bloomington, IN

"So simple, yet extraordinarily delicious."

Gayle

keep it hot

If you're taking a casserole to a potluck dinner or picnic, keep it toasty by covering the casserole dish with foil and then wrapping it in several layers of newspaper.

rice pilaf with carrots

Toasting brings out the full flavor of nuts. Toast the pine nuts in a dry skillet over medium heat for just a few minutes, stirring often.

1 T. vegetable oil
2 c. basmati rice, uncooked
¼ c. onion, chopped
2 cloves garlic, minced
4 c. chicken broth

½ t. salt
1 c. carrots, peeled and finely
   chopped
½ c. green onions, chopped
3 T. pine nuts, toasted

Heat oil in a medium saucepan over medium-high heat. Add rice and onion; sauté 2 minutes. Add garlic; sauté one minute. Add broth and salt; bring to a boil. Cover, reduce heat and simmer 7 minutes. Stir in carrots; cover and cook 7 more minutes or until liquid is absorbed. Remove from heat; stir in green onions and toasted pine nuts. Let stand, covered, 15 minutes; fluff with a fork. Serves 6 to 8.

risotto in the microwave

(pictured on page 312)

Microwave risotto takes about the same amount of time to prepare as traditional risotto, though most of its preparation is hands off, giving you more time for cooking the rest of your dinner.

2 T. butter
2 T. olive oil
½ c. onion, minced
1 c. Arborio rice

3 c. reduced-sodium chicken broth
½ c. grated Parmesan cheese
¼ t. pepper

Microwave butter and oil, uncovered, in a microwave-safe 1½-quart glass or ceramic dish on high for one minute and 15 seconds to 2 minutes. Add onion; stir well. Cover and cook on high 45 seconds to one minute. Add rice, stirring well. Cover and cook on high 3 to 4 minutes. Stir in chicken broth; cook, uncovered, on high 9 minutes. Stir well, and cook, uncovered, on high 7 minutes. Remove from microwave oven and let stand 5 minutes. Stir in Parmesan cheese and pepper. Makes 3½ cups.

company rice

(pictured on page 308)

Today's grocery stores carry a variety of quick-cooking wild rice blends…choose one if you want a quicker-cooking substitute.

¼ c. butter, cut into pieces
6-oz. pkg. wild rice
8-oz. pkg. sliced mushrooms
14½-oz. can chicken broth
3 green onions, chopped

½ t. salt
Optional: 2 T. dry sherry
Optional: ½ c. sliced almonds,
  toasted

Melt butter in a 2-quart saucepan over medium heat. Stir in rice; cook 5 minutes, stirring occasionally. Add mushrooms, next 3 ingredients and sherry, if desired; bring to a boil. Cover, reduce heat and simmer one hour and 5 minutes or until rice is done; drain excess liquid, if desired. Fluff rice with a fork; sprinkle with almonds, if desired. Serves 8.

make-ahead slow-cooker method: company rice

Combine first 6 ingredients and, if desired, sherry in a 4-quart electric slow cooker; cover and cook on high setting 3 hours. Drain excess liquid, if necessary. Fluff rice with a fork; sprinkle with almonds, if desired.

honey-kissed acorn squash

Select acorn squash that's firm, unblemished and feels heavy for its size. A cut squash will keep in the fridge up to one week. Uncut, it will stay fresh for one month in a cool, dark place.

2 acorn squash, halved lengthwise
   and seeded
8-oz. can crushed pineapple, drained
¼ c. chopped pecans

¼ c. sweetened dried cranberries
¼ c. plus 2 T. honey
¼ c. butter, melted
Optional: ground nutmeg

Place squash halves, cut-side up, in a microwave-safe dish; microwave on high for 8 to 10 minutes until tender. Combine pineapple and next 4 ingredients; spoon into squash halves. Microwave on high 30 to 45 seconds or until thoroughly heated and lightly glazed. Sprinkle with nutmeg, if desired. Serves 4.

Lynda McCormick
Burkburnett, TX

"This winter squash is a fresh side dish that makes a great addition to any dinner menu."

Lynda

praline-topped butternut squash

Walnuts replace pecans in this buttery, sweet topping. The squash is a tasty substitute for sweet potato casserole on any fall menu.

2 butternut squash, peeled and
   cubed
7 T. butter, divided
½ t. salt
⅛ t. pepper

2 eggs, beaten
½ c. brown sugar, packed
½ c. chopped walnuts
½ t. cinnamon
⅛ t. ground nutmeg

Boil squash in water to cover until soft; drain.

Process squash in a blender until smooth. Transfer to a saucepan; stir in 4 tablespoons butter, salt and pepper. Heat thoroughly; remove from heat.

Stir in eggs; spread into a greased one-quart baking dish. Set aside. Combine brown sugar, walnuts, cinnamon, nutmeg and remaining 3 tablespoons butter; sprinkle over squash mixture. Bake at 350 degrees for 30 minutes. Serves 8.

Nancy Kowalski
Southbury, CT

family comfort

When I was growing up, my very special friend was my Grammy. She lived with us for ten years when she first came to America from Hungary in 1946. Our best times together were when she would cook or bake. I was always fascinated because she never used a recipe and could whip up anything!

I learned her recipes by watching and touching. She made many comfort foods, but the greatest comfort was her friendship of sharing, caring and spending time with me.

Susie Knupp
Somers, MT

squash casserole
(pictured on page 2)

Yellow squash is also known as crookneck squash because of its thin, curved neck. You can substitute equal amounts of zucchini in this recipe, if you prefer.

2½ lbs. yellow squash, sliced
½ c. butter
14-oz. jar diced pimento, drained
½ c. onion, chopped
2 eggs, beaten
¼ c. green pepper, chopped
¼ c. mayonnaise

2 t. sugar
1½ t. salt
Optional: 8-oz. can sliced water
    chestnuts, drained and chopped
10 round buttery crackers, crushed
½ c. shredded sharp Cheddar cheese

Cook squash, covered, in a small amount of boiling water 8 to 10 minutes or until tender; drain well, pressing between paper towels.

Combine squash and butter in a bowl; mash until butter melts. Stir in pimento, next 6 ingredients and water chestnuts, if desired; spoon into a lightly greased shallow 2-quart baking dish. Sprinkle with crushed crackers.

Bake at 325 degrees for 30 minutes. Sprinkle with cheese; bake 5 more minutes or until cheese melts. Serves 8.

tomato pie

Vine-ripened tomatoes are ideal for this summer pie...what flavor!

9-inch unbaked pie crust
1 c. shredded mozzarella cheese,
    divided
4 tomatoes, seeded and chopped
1 onion, chopped

10 to 12 fresh basil leaves, chopped
1 c. shredded Cheddar cheese
1 c. mayonnaise
½ c. grated Parmesan cheese

Prick bottom of pie crust several times with the tines of a fork; bake at 425 degrees for 8 to 10 minutes.

Sprinkle bottom of pie crust with ¼ cup mozzarella cheese. Layer with half each of tomatoes, onion and basil; repeat layers. Combine ¾ cup mozzarella cheese, Cheddar cheese and mayonnaise. Spread mixture over top of pie; sprinkle with Parmesan cheese. Bake at 350 degrees on bottom rack of oven for 35 to 40 minutes. Let stand 15 minutes before serving. Serves 6.

Shelia Willis
Annapolis, MD

"Grow your own tomatoes and basil this year and use them in this tasty tomato pie!"

Shelia

spicy grilled vegetables

Place the vegetables directly on the grill for true smoky flavor.

4 potatoes, sliced diagonally
3 large carrots, peeled and sliced
  lengthwise
2 large zucchini, sliced crosswise
2 T. onion, chopped

⅓ c. olive oil
1 T. lime juice
½ t. salt
½ t. ground cumin
¼ t. pepper

Place potatoes and carrots in a medium saucepan and cover with water. Boil 10 minutes over high heat. Drain and place in a large bowl; add zucchini slices.

Combine onion and next 5 ingredients in a small bowl. Pour over vegetables, tossing to coat well. Let stand about 15 minutes, allowing flavors to blend. Grill vegetables over medium-high heat (350 to 400 degrees) for about 3 minutes on each side, turning once. Serve hot. Serves 4 to 6.

eat your veggies!

Get kids to eat their vegetables! Serve fresh cut-up vegetables with small cups of creamy salad dressing or even peanut butter for dipping.

stuffed zucchini

Zucchini is so plentiful that new recipes are always welcome…especially tasty ones like this.

½ c. bread crumbs

2 T. grated Parmesan cheese

4 T. butter, divided

½ c. onion, chopped

1 clove garlic, minced

1 tomato, peeled and chopped

2 zucchini, halved, scooped out
    and pulp and shells reserved

salt and pepper to taste

Toss together bread crumbs, cheese and 2 tablespoons butter in a small dish. Sauté onion and garlic in remaining 2 tablespoons butter until tender. Add tomato and zucchini pulp; mix well and heat thoroughly.

Place zucchini shells in a greased baking dish; fill with stuffing. Top with bread crumb mixture; bake, covered, at 350 degrees for 30 minutes. Season with salt and pepper to taste and serve immediately. Serves 4.

Roasted Veggie Panini, page 180,
and Cream of Chicken-Rice Soup, page 169

soups,
sandwiches & salads

Whether served alone or paired together, soups, sandwiches &

salads are ideal for lunch or supper. Chicken Stew with Biscuits

(page 176) beckons to be served on a cold, blustery day, while

Chicken, Artichoke & Rice Salad (page 196) is just right for a

springtime luncheon. Whatever the season or occasion, favorites

like Roasted Veggie Panini (page 180), Colorful

Couscous Salad (page 195) and others inside

this chapter are just perfect for sharing with

family & friends.

curried harvest bisque

To make peeling and cutting butternut squash a little easier, microwave it on high for one minute.

1 lb. butternut squash, peeled and cut into 1-inch cubes	1 t. curry powder
5 c. chicken broth	¾ c. half-and-half
¼ c. butter	1 T. lime juice
¼ c. all-purpose flour	½ t. salt
	¼ t. white pepper

Combine squash and broth in a heavy 4-quart stockpot. Cook about 15 minutes over medium heat until tender. Using a slotted spoon, transfer squash to a blender or food processor; process until smooth. Stir broth into puréed squash; set aside.

Melt butter in stockpot; stir in flour and curry powder. Cook over medium heat, stirring until smooth. Add squash mixture; increase heat to medium-high and stir until soup thickens slightly. Reduce heat to low; add half-and-half and remaining ingredients and heat thoroughly (do not boil). Serves 6.

Kathy Grashoff
Fort Wayne, IN

cream of chicken-rice soup

(pictured on page 166)

Don't let a cold be the only reason you serve up this chicken soup…it's perfect year 'round!

4 qts. water
2 boneless, skinless chicken breasts
2 carrots, chopped
2 ribs celery, chopped
1 onion, chopped
¼ c. fresh parsley, minced

¼ c. butter
2 cloves garlic, minced
1 c. rice, uncooked
2 t. salt
2 c. milk
½ c. cornstarch

Bring water to a boil in a Dutch oven. Add chicken and cook until done. Remove chicken from broth to cool, reserving broth in Dutch oven.

Meanwhile, sauté carrots, celery, onion and parsley in butter in a large skillet until tender. Add garlic and cook one minute. Cut chicken into bite-size pieces. Add sautéed vegetables and chicken to reserved broth. Stir in rice and salt and simmer 15 minutes. Mix together milk and cornstarch; add to soup. Stir until thickened. Serves 16 to 20.

Michelle Heurung
Mokena, IL

"Prepare this creamy soup and watch it disappear!"

Michelle

chicken fajita chowder

This chunky chowder is full of Mexican flavor! Serve it with a variety of tortilla chips for an added burst of color.

3 T. all-purpose flour
1.4-oz. pkg. fajita or taco seasoning
    mix, divided
4 boneless, skinless chicken breasts,
    cubed
3 T. vegetable oil
1 onion, chopped
1 t. garlic, minced
15¼-oz. can sweet corn and diced
    peppers, drained
15-oz. can black beans, drained and
    rinsed

14½-oz. can Mexican-style stewed
    tomatoes
4.5-oz. can chopped green chiles
3 c. water
1 c. instant brown rice, uncooked
10¾-oz. can nacho cheese soup
1¼ c. water
Toppings: sour cream, shredded
    Cheddar cheese, chopped green
    onions, tortilla chips
Garnish: fresh cilantro sprigs

Combine flour and 2 tablespoons seasoning mix in a large plastic zipping bag; add chicken. Seal bag and shake to coat. Sauté chicken in hot oil in a large Dutch oven over high heat about 5 minutes or until golden, stirring often.

Reduce heat to medium-high. Add onion and garlic; sauté 5 minutes. Stir in remaining seasoning mix, corn and next 5 ingredients; bring to a boil. Reduce heat to medium-low; cover and simmer 5 minutes. Add soup and 1¼ cups water; stir until thoroughly heated. Sprinkle with desired toppings; garnish, if desired. Serves 8 to 10.

Kelly Jones
Tallahassee, FL

"This takes a bit of time to prepare, but it's well worth it. You'll have a savory soup that will be a new family favorite."

Kelly

baked potato soup

If your favorite baked potato toppings aren't listed, feel free to add them!

3 lbs. redskin potatoes, cubed
¼ c. butter
¼ c. all-purpose flour
2 qts. half-and-half
16-oz. pkg. pasteurized process
   cheese spread, cubed

1 t. hot pepper sauce
white pepper and garlic
   powder to taste
Toppings: crumbled bacon,
   shredded Cheddar cheese,
   snipped fresh chives

Cover potatoes with water in a large saucepan; bring to a boil. Boil
10 minutes or until tender; drain and set aside.

Melt butter in a large Dutch oven; add flour, stirring until smooth. Gradually add half-and-half, stirring constantly over low heat. Continue to stir until
smooth and mixture begins to thicken. Add cheese; stir well. Add potatoes,
hot pepper sauce and seasonings. Cover and simmer over low heat 30 minutes.
Sprinkle with desired toppings. Serves 8.

Linda Stone
Cookeville, TN

creamy white chili

(pictured on page 312)

Sour cream and whipping cream are stirred into this chili, making it extra rich and creamy. Rotate white chili into your menu as a substitute for chili with beef and kidney beans.

1 T. vegetable oil
1 lb. boneless, skinless chicken
  breast, cubed
1 onion, chopped
14-oz. can chicken broth
2 (15.8-oz.) cans Great Northern
  beans, drained and rinsed
2 (4.5-oz.) cans chopped green
  chiles, undrained

1½ t. garlic powder
1 t. salt
1 t. ground cumin
½ t. dried oregano
8-oz. container sour cream
1 c. whipping cream
2 c. shredded Monterey Jack cheese
Garnish: cilantro sprigs

Heat oil in a large skillet over medium heat; add chicken and onion. Sauté 10 minutes or until chicken is done; set aside.

Combine broth, beans, chiles and seasonings in a large Dutch oven. Bring to a boil over medium-high heat. Add chicken mixture; reduce heat and simmer 30 minutes. Add sour cream and whipping cream, stirring well. Top each serving with shredded cheese; garnish, if desired. Serves 6 to 8.

Janelle Dixon
Fernley, NV

"This chili has such a fabulous flavor with its blend of green chiles, cumin, sour cream and chicken."

Janelle

optional toppings

It's the unexpected touches that make the biggest impression. When serving soup or chili, offer guests a variety of fun toppings…fill bowls with shredded cheese, oyster crackers, chopped onions, sour cream and crunchy croutons. Then invite everyone to dig in!

vegetarian Cincinnati chili

Here's a meatless version of a traditional dish in Cincinnati, where chili lovers order their chili by numbers. Serve it over cooked spaghetti for 2-way chili or topped with shredded cheese for 3-way chili. Topping it with chopped raw onions makes it 4-way, while a sprinkling of extra beans takes it to 5-way. We show our chili at left as 3-way, since onions and beans are already part of this meatless version.

46-oz. can tomato juice
2 (15-oz.) cans kidney beans,
    drained and rinsed
15-oz. can black beans, drained
    and rinsed
1 onion, chopped
2 T. chili powder
1½ t. white vinegar
1 t. allspice

1 t. cinnamon
1 t. pepper
1 t. ground cumin
¼ t. Worcestershire sauce
⅛ t. garlic powder
5 bay leaves
Optional: cooked spaghetti,
    shredded Cheddar cheese,
    oyster crackers

Combine first 13 ingredients in a 3-quart slow cooker. Cover and cook on low setting 5 hours. Discard bay leaves before serving. If desired, serve over cooked spaghetti; sprinkle with cheese and serve with oyster crackers. Serves 6.

Leath Sarvo
Cincinnati, OH

chicken stew with biscuits

(pictured on page 313)

Your meat, veggies and bread are all combined in one hearty stew!

2 c. water
¾ c. dry white wine or chicken
  broth
2 (.87-oz.) pkgs. chicken gravy mix
2 cloves garlic, minced
1 T. fresh parsley, minced
1 to 2 t. chicken bouillon granules
½ t. pepper
5 small carrots, peeled and cut into
  1-inch pieces

4 boneless, skinless chicken breasts,
  cut into bite-size pieces
1 onion, cut into 8 wedges
3 T. all-purpose flour
⅓ c. cold water
black pepper to taste
16.3-oz. tube refrigerated large
  buttermilk biscuits, baked

Combine first 7 ingredients in a 3½- or 4-quart slow cooker; stir until blended. Add carrots, chicken and onion; cover and cook on high setting one hour. Reduce heat to low setting and cook 3 to 4 hours.

Stir together flour and cold water until smooth in a small bowl. Gradually stir into slow cooker; cover and cook one more hour. Pour stew into individual soup bowls; sprinkle with black pepper, if desired, and top with biscuits. Serves 4 to 6.

Debi Piper
Vicksburg, MI

chicken-andouille gumbo

We cut in half the time that it takes to stir up a good roux by first browning it in the oven. It's finished off in a skillet using less oil than normal, but the flavor still maintains its richness.

1½ gal. water

4-lb. chicken, cut up

5 bay leaves

5 sprigs parsley

3 cloves garlic

1 lb. andouille or smoked sausage, diced

2 onions, chopped

1 large green pepper, chopped

1 large rib celery, chopped

3 T. garlic, minced

4 chicken bouillon cubes

1½ c. all-purpose flour

¾ c. vegetable oil

1 T. salt

1 t. cayenne pepper

1 t. black pepper

1 bunch green onions, chopped

½ c. fresh parsley, chopped

½ t. filé powder

hot cooked rice

Bring first 5 ingredients to a boil in a large stockpot; cover, reduce heat and simmer one hour. Remove chicken, reserving broth. Skin, bone and coarsely chop chicken; set aside.

Pour broth through a wire-mesh strainer into a large bowl, discarding solids. Measure one gallon broth and return to stockpot. Add sausage and next 5 ingredients; simmer one hour, stirring occasionally.

Meanwhile, place flour in a 15"x10" jelly-roll pan. Bake at 400 degrees for 10 to 15 minutes or until flour is a caramel color, stirring every 5 minutes.

Heat oil in a heavy skillet over medium heat; gradually whisk in browned flour and cook, whisking constantly, until flour is a dark caramel color (about 7 minutes). Stir into sausage mixture and simmer one hour, stirring occasionally. Stir in chicken, salt and cayenne and black pepper; simmer 45 minutes, stirring occasionally.

Stir in green onions and parsley; simmer 10 minutes, stirring occasionally. Remove from heat and stir in filé powder. Serve over hot cooked rice. Serves 12.

mamma mia Italian stew

This stew is chock-full of flavorful summer produce with a hint of heat from hot Italian sausage.

1 lb. ground hot Italian sausage,
    cooked and drained
1 eggplant, peeled and cubed
1½ c. sliced green beans
2 green peppers, sliced
1 to 2 potatoes, peeled and cubed
1 large zucchini, cubed

1 large yellow squash, cubed
1 c. onion, thinly sliced
15-oz. can Italian-style
    tomato sauce
¼ c. olive oil
2 t. garlic, minced
1 t. salt

Combine all ingredients in a 7-quart slow cooker; stir well. Cover and cook on low setting 8 hours or on high setting 4 hours. Serves 8 to 10.

Connie Bryant
Topeka, KS

seasonal menus

Thinking of a menu for guests? Let the season be your guide! Soups and stews brimming with the harvest's bounty are just right for fall get-togethers, and juicy fruit salads are delightful in the summer. Not only will you get the freshest ingredients when you plan by the season, but you'll also get the best prices at the supermarket!

roasted veggie panini
(pictured on page 166)

If you don't have a panini press, place the sandwiches in a hot skillet and gently press them with a smaller heavy pan; cook over medium-low heat until the cheese melts.

2 zucchini, sliced
1 yellow squash, sliced
6 oz. portobello mushroom caps, sliced
2 t. olive oil, divided
1 t. balsamic vinegar
1 sweet onion, thinly sliced
1 loaf sourdough bread, sliced

¼ c. olive tapénade
1 red pepper, sliced into rings
1 green pepper, sliced into rings
1 yellow pepper, sliced into rings
1 c. spinach leaves
2 roma tomatoes, sliced
4 slices provolone cheese

Combine zucchini, squash and mushrooms in a large bowl; toss with one teaspoon olive oil and vinegar. Grill, covered, over medium-high heat (350 to 400 degrees) 15 to 20 minutes, turning occasionally; set aside.

Heat one teaspoon olive oil in a skillet over medium heat. Add onion and cook 15 minutes or until caramelized, stirring often; set aside.

Spread tops and bottoms of bread slices with olive tapénade; layer red pepper rings and next 5 ingredients evenly on half the bread slices and top with remaining bread slices. Preheat panini press according to manufacturer's instructions. Place sandwiches in press (in batches, if necessary); cook 3 to 4 minutes or until cheese melts and bread is toasted. Serves 4.

Note: Look for olive tapénade in the deli section of larger supermarkets.

Lynda McCormick
Burkburnett, TX

Greek salad in a pita pocket

You can make a delicious sandwich by stuffing tasty pita bread with almost any vegetable salad. Some pita bread is made with whole wheat, providing extra nutrients in your meal.

1 red pepper, thinly sliced
½ avocado, pitted and sliced
¼ sweet red onion, thinly sliced
5 to 6 black Greek olives, pitted and
    sliced
crumbled feta cheese to taste

1 t. garlic, crushed
fresh dill, chopped, to taste
½ t. dried oregano
oil and vinegar salad dressing to
    taste
4 rounds pita bread, split

Gently toss first 8 ingredients with dressing in a medium bowl. Stuff mixture into pita pockets. Serves 4.

sandwich smorgasbord

Whip up several different kinds of sandwiches (or stop at the local deli for a few!) and cut each one into 4 sections. Arrange them all on a large platter with chips and pickles…everyone will love the variety, and the preparation couldn't be easier.

dressed oyster po'boys

This loaf is piled high with plump fried oysters and slaw…all atop a tangy sauce. Mmm…it's good!

1¼ c. self-rising cornmeal

2 T. salt-free Creole seasoning

2 (12-oz.) containers fresh Standard
 oysters, drained

peanut or vegetable oil

1 c. mayonnaise, divided

2 T. Dijon mustard

2 T. white vinegar

6 c. finely shredded multi-colored
 cabbage

2 T. catsup

1 T. prepared horseradish

1 t. salt-free Creole seasoning

¾ t. paprika

4 hoagie rolls, split and toasted

Combine cornmeal and Creole seasoning; dredge oysters in mixture.

Pour oil to a depth of 2 inches into a Dutch oven; heat to 375 degrees. Fry oysters, in 3 batches, 2 to 3 minutes or until golden. Drain on wire racks.

Stir together ½ cup mayonnaise, mustard and vinegar. Stir in cabbage; set slaw aside.

Stir together remaining ½ cup mayonnaise, catsup and next 3 ingredients.

Spread bottom halves of rolls with mayonnaise mixture. Layer with oysters and top with slaw; cover with roll tops. Serves 4.

Italian sausage sandwiches
(pictured on page 311)

*The sausages are flavored with garlic and fennel seeds and are available sweet
or hot. Let your taste buds lead you to your choice.*

8 Italian sausages
1 Bermuda or Spanish onion,
   chopped
2 green peppers, quartered
   and sliced
1 t. salt
1 t. sugar

1 t. Italian seasoning
Optional: 2 tomatoes, chopped
8 hoagie rolls
4 t. butter, divided
16-oz. pkg. shredded mozzarella
   cheese, divided

Score the sausages every ½ inch. Cook sausages in a large skillet
15 minutes or until browned and cooked through; drain on paper towels.
Pour off drippings, reserving 3 tablespoons drippings; place reserved drippings
back into skillet.

Add onion to skillet and sauté until tender. Stir in green peppers, salt, sugar
and Italian seasoning. Cover and cook 5 minutes; stir in tomatoes, if desired.
Place sausages on top. Cook, covered, 5 minutes or until mixture bubbles.

Meanwhile, cut out center of rolls to make boat-shaped shells. Spread
½ teaspoon butter on the inside of each roll; place rolls on a baking sheet and
bake at 350 degrees for 10 minutes. Divide mozzarella cheese evenly among
hoagie rolls. Place one sausage in each roll; top with onion mixture. Serves 8.

Joanne Ciancio
Silver Lake, OH

salami submarine with olive salad

The olive salad improves with age and is delicious on other sandwiches as well.

18-inch loaf crusty French bread
Olive Salad

¼ lb. Genoa salami, thinly sliced
¼ lb. Swiss cheese, thinly sliced

Slice bread lengthwise but do not cut all the way through to the other side. Scoop out some of the bread from inside of each half. Pack Olive Salad evenly into each half. Layer salami and cheese in rows down each half of sandwich. Close the halves together and wrap tightly in heavy aluminum foil. Slice to serve. Serves 6 to 8.

olive salad:

3 c. green and black olives, coarsely
   chopped
7-oz. jar roasted red peppers,
   drained and chopped
½ c. fresh parsley, chopped

¼ c. fresh basil, chopped
6 T. olive oil
3 T. red wine vinegar
2 T. capers
2 cloves garlic, crushed

Toss together all ingredients in a large bowl and store in a tightly covered glass jar in the refrigerator.

heat it up

Bake your foil-wrapped sub at 350 degrees for 20 minutes, then unwrap and sprinkle Italian dressing inside the bun for a hot, crisp treat. For extra tang, add banana peppers.

pepperoni calzones

To save time, prepare this dish using refrigerated pizza dough.

1 c. water
1 pkg. active dry yeast
3 c. all-purpose flour
1 T. sugar
2 T. canola oil
1 t. salt

Tomato-Basil Sauce
1½ c. green pepper, chopped
1½ c. shredded mozzarella cheese
1½ c. sliced pepperoni
1 egg, beaten

Heat water until very warm (100 to 110 degrees). Dissolve yeast in warm water; set aside for 5 minutes. Combine one cup flour, sugar, oil and salt in a large mixing bowl; beat at low speed with an electric mixer until blended. Gradually stir in enough remaining flour to make a smooth dough. Turn dough out onto a lightly floured surface; knead until smooth and elastic (8 to 10 minutes). Place in a well-greased bowl, turning to grease top. Cover and let rise in a warm place (85 degrees), free from drafts, 30 minutes or until doubled in bulk.

Punch dough down; divide into 6 equal portions. Roll each portion into a 7-inch circle. Divide one cup Tomato-Basil Sauce evenly over each circle, spreading to within one inch of edge. Sprinkle one half of each circle evenly with green pepper, cheese and pepperoni. Fold each circle in half to cover filling and pinch edges to seal. Place on an ungreased baking sheet; let rest 15 minutes. Brush with egg; bake at 375 degrees for 20 minutes. Serve with remaining Tomato-Basil Sauce. Serves 6.

tomato-basil sauce:

15-oz. can tomato sauce
½ c. tomato paste
2 t. dried basil

2 t. dried oregano
2 cloves garlic, minced
8-oz. pkg. sliced mushrooms

Combine first 5 ingredients; mix well. Divide in half; stir mushrooms into half of sauce to use in calzones. Serve calzones with remaining sauce. Makes 2 cups.

Amy Greer
Elkhart, IN

French dip sandwiches

This brisket is tenderized during its long cook time in the slow cooker. Invite family & friends over to enjoy these savory sandwiches…they feed a crowd!

6 lbs. beef brisket
¼ c. mesquite-flavored cooking
    sauce
2 cloves garlic, pressed
½ t. dry mustard
½ t. seasoning salt
½ t. flavor enhancer
½ t. meat tenderizer

½ t. ground cumin
½ t. pepper
¼ t. onion powder
¼ t. cayenne pepper
¼ t. dried marjoram
¼ t. dried tarragon
2 (10½-oz.) cans beef broth
12 French rolls, toasted

Cut brisket in half; place in a 6- to 7-quart slow cooker. Combine cooking sauce and next 11 ingredients; stir well. Pour mixture over brisket; cover and cook on high setting one hour. Reduce heat to low setting and cook 8 hours.

Remove meat from slow cooker, reserving broth. Skim a few ice cubes across the surface of broth to remove fat, if desired, and discard. Cool brisket slightly and cut into slices; return meat to broth in slow cooker. Add canned beef broth. Increase to high setting and cook 30 to 45 minutes or until meat and liquid are thoroughly heated. Serve on French rolls with a small serving of broth on the side for dipping. Serves 12.

Denise Collins
Canyon Country, CA

giant meatball sandwich

The combination of ground pork and ground chuck enhances the flavor of these meatballs. If you're pinched for time, though, use already-prepared meatballs, which you can find in your grocer's freezer.

1 lb. ground chuck
½ lb. ground pork sausage
2 c. spaghetti sauce with peppers
  and mushrooms
1 clove garlic, minced
1-lb. loaf unsliced Italian bread
6-oz. pkg. sliced provolone cheese

Combine ground chuck and sausage; shape into one-inch balls. Cook meatballs in a large skillet over medium-high heat 8 to 10 minutes or until browned. Drain meatballs on paper towels. Discard drippings.

Combine meatballs, spaghetti sauce and garlic in skillet; bring to a boil. Reduce heat and simmer, uncovered, 12 to 15 minutes or until meatballs are done, stirring mixture occasionally.

While sauce simmers, slice bread in half lengthwise. Place bread, cut-side up, on a baking sheet. Broil 5½ inches from heat one to 2 minutes or until bread is lightly toasted. Spoon meatball mixture over bottom half of toasted bread; arrange cheese on top of meatballs, overlapping as needed. Cover with top of bread. Cut sandwich into 6 pieces; serve immediately. Serves 6.

quick solutions

Easiest-ever sandwiches for a get-together…provide a big platter of cold cuts, a basket of fresh breads and a choice of condiments so guests can make their own. Add cups of hot soup plus cookies for dessert…done!

open-faced Philly sandwiches

These sandwiches are great by themselves, but you could add a salad or home fries for a side dish, if you'd like.

3 (8-inch) submarine rolls, unsliced
½ lb. boneless top round steak
2 T. Italian salad dressing
¼ t. red pepper flakes
2 T. butter

1 large onion, thinly sliced
1 green pepper, cut into thin strips
1½ c. sliced mushrooms
1 clove garlic, pressed
1 c. shredded provolone cheese

Make a 1½-inch to 2-inch deep vertical cut around outside edges of each roll, leaving a ½-inch border. Remove tops of rolls and discard. Hollow out about 1½ inches of each bread roll, forming a boat. Set boats aside.

Cut steak diagonally across grain into ⅛-inch-thick strips; place in a small shallow bowl. Add dressing and red pepper flakes, tossing to coat; set aside.

Melt butter in a non-stick skillet over medium-high heat; add onion, green pepper and mushrooms and sauté 15 minutes or until onion is golden brown. Add garlic and sauté one minute. Remove mixture from skillet and set aside.

Stir-fry steak mixture in skillet over medium-high heat 2 to 3 minutes or until steak strips are no longer pink.

Fill bread boats evenly with layers of steak mixture and onion mixture; top with cheese.

Broil 5½ inches from heat 3 minutes or until cheese is lightly browned. Serves 3.

the best salad

Oregano and garlic are tasty additions to the homemade croutons that are part of this recipe. Season them according to your family's taste, and you'll have a winner however you flavor them.

3 to 4 slices day-old bread, crusts trimmed
1-lb. pkg. bacon, crisply cooked and crumbled, drippings reserved
⅓ c. sugar
⅓ c. white vinegar
3 egg yolks

8-oz. container sour cream
1 to 2 T. butter
seasonings or herbs to taste
1 head romaine lettuce, torn into bite-size pieces
4 to 5 green onions, chopped

Cut bread into cubes; set aside. Heat 2 tablespoons reserved bacon drippings in skillet; stir together sugar and vinegar and add to skillet. Bring mixture to a boil; boil about 5 minutes.

Blend together egg yolks and sour cream in a small bowl. Add to skillet; cook over medium heat about 7 minutes, stirring constantly, until mixture thickens.

Melt butter in a saucepan and add seasonings to taste for croutons; toss bread cubes to coat. Spread bread cubes on a large ungreased baking sheet and bake at 350 degrees for 10 to 15 minutes or until golden. Arrange lettuce in a large salad bowl; pour hot dressing over top. Sprinkle with crumbled bacon, croutons and green onions. Toss before serving. Serves 4.

Taylor Driscoll
Beaver Crossing, NE

Parmesan-chicken salad

Serve this versatile salad over lettuce, as a sandwich or by itself with crackers…it's delicious any way you choose.

4 boneless, skinless chicken breasts
1 t. salt
½ t. pepper
2 T. vegetable oil
¾ c. shredded Parmesan cheese
¾ c. mayonnaise

½ c. chopped pecans, toasted
½ c. celery, chopped
⅓ c. green onions, chopped
1 clove garlic, pressed
2 T. spicy brown mustard

Sprinkle chicken with salt and pepper. Cook chicken in hot oil in a large skillet over medium-high heat 7 to 8 minutes on each side or until done; cool.

Chop chicken. Stir together chicken, cheese and remaining ingredients. Cover and chill at least 2 hours. Serves 4.

a new twist

Use old serving dishes in a new way for a fresh look. Handed-down cream-and-sugar sets can hold sauces, bread sticks can be arranged in gravy boats and a trifle dish can make a great salad bowl.

colorful couscous salad

Couscous is actually a tiny pasta, but it's found in the rice section of supermarkets. It cooks up quickly and is a nice alternative to rice.

10-oz. box couscous, cooked
1 green pepper, diced
1 bunch green onions, diced
4 carrots, shredded
15½-oz. can black beans,
    drained and rinsed
15¼-oz. can whole kernel corn,
    drained
¾ c. olive oil
¼ c. lemon juice
⅛ c. white wine vinegar

2 T. sugar
1 T. garlic, minced
3 drops hot pepper sauce
½ t. salt
½ t. pepper
½ t. lemon-pepper seasoning
½ t. seasoned salt
¼ t. ground turmeric
⅛ t. cinnamon
⅛ t. ground ginger

Fluff couscous in a large bowl. Add green pepper and remaining ingredients, stirring well. Refrigerate until ready to serve. Serves 6 to 8.

Donna Cash
Dexter, MI

> "Look for flavored couscous in the rice aisle...so tasty and easy!"
>
> Donna

edible "bowls"

Serve up individual portions of this colorful dish in edible bowls! Hollow out fresh green or red peppers and fill 'em up with salad for a tasty lunch.

chicken, artichoke & rice salad
(pictured on page 306)

This salad pairs nicely with Raspberry Scones (page 211) for a simple luncheon with friends.

6.9-oz. pkg. chicken-flavored rice
   vermicelli mix, cooked
2 c. diced cooked chicken
6-oz. jar marinated quartered
   artichoke hearts, liquid reserved
1 green pepper, chopped
1 bunch green onions, chopped

8-oz. can water chestnuts, drained
   and chopped
⅔ c. mayonnaise
½ t. curry powder
⅛ t. salt
⅛ t. pepper

    Combine rice vermicelli mix and chicken in a serving bowl. Add artichoke hearts and reserved liquid to rice mixture. Add green pepper and remaining ingredients; chill before serving. Serves 3 to 4.

Charlotte Mitchell
Anchorage, AK

memories of friends

    Thumbing through the index cards in my little wooden recipe box is more than just a search for something good to eat. Among those smudged and often yellowed cards, there's a history of family & friends.

Pat Ockert
Jonesboro, AR

frosty fruit salad

Roll some fresh grapes, strawberries and mandarin oranges in extra-fine sugar for a glittery (and tasty!) garnish.

17-oz. can apricots, chopped and
    juice reserved
17-oz. can crushed pineapple, juice
    reserved
½ c. sugar
3 (10-oz.) pkgs. frozen strawberries,
    thawed

6-oz. can frozen orange juice
    concentrate
2 T. lemon juice
2 lbs. grapes, halved
4 bananas, diced

Heat reserved juices and sugar in a heavy saucepan over medium heat; stir until sugar dissolves. Add strawberries, orange juice concentrate and lemon juice. Heat until warmed; remove from heat. Combine apricots, pineapple, grapes and bananas in a large bowl; add juice mixture and toss to coat fruit. Pour into a freezer-safe serving dish; freeze overnight. Remove from freezer about 15 to 25 minutes before serving. Serves 25 to 30.

Lisa Smith
Littleton, CO

"Made the night before, it's just right for after-noon picnics!"

Lisa

cranberry-Gorgonzola green salad

Tart dried cranberries and Gorgonzola contribute outstanding flavor to this green salad. For variety, add half each of a Granny Smith apple and your favorite crisp red apple. For a colorful combination, don't peel them.

⅓ c. vegetable oil
¼ c. seasoned rice vinegar
¾ t. Dijon mustard
1 clove garlic, pressed
1 small head Bibb lettuce, torn
1 small head green leaf lettuce, torn

1 apple, chopped
⅓ c. coarsely chopped walnuts, toasted
⅓ c. dried cranberries
⅓ c. crumbled Gorgonzola cheese

Whisk together first 4 ingredients in a small bowl; set aside.

Just before serving, combine Bibb lettuce and next 5 ingredients in a large bowl. Pour dressing over salad; toss gently. Serves 8.

glass milk bottles

Antique bottles make fun containers for serving salad dressings. Fill each with a different variety of dressing and set them around the table, or place filled bottles in a wire milk carrier…clever!

green bean salad with feta

Crumbled feta cheese, toasted walnuts and a sliced red onion make up the basic ingredients for this green bean salad. Leave the green beans whole for a pretty presentation.

¾ c. olive oil
¼ c. white wine vinegar
1 clove garlic, minced
½ t. salt
¼ t. pepper

2 lbs. small green beans
1 small red onion, thinly sliced
4-oz. pkg. crumbled feta cheese
1 c. coarsely chopped walnuts,
  toasted

Whisk together first 5 ingredients in a small bowl; set aside.

Trim stem end of green beans; cut or snap beans into thirds, if desired, and arrange in a steamer basket over boiling water. Cover and steam 8 to 12 minutes or until crisp-tender. Immediately plunge beans into cold water to stop the cooking process; drain and pat dry.

Combine beans, onion and cheese in a large bowl; toss well. Pour oil mixture over bean mixture; cover and chill one hour. Add walnuts just before serving and toss gently. Serves 8.

blue cheese potato salad

Try a variation of this recipe with new potatoes…no need to peel. Garnish with fresh dill.

3½ to 4 lbs. redskin potatoes,
   peeled, boiled and cubed
½ c. scallions, chopped
½ c. celery, chopped
2 T. fresh parsley, chopped
½ c. slivered almonds, toasted

2 t. salt
½ t. celery seed
¼ t. pepper
2 c. sour cream
½ c. crumbled blue cheese
¼ c. white wine vinegar

Combine potatoes, scallions, celery, parsley, almonds, salt, celery seed, and pepper in a large bowl. Mix together sour cream, blue cheese and vinegar in another bowl. Pour over potato mixture and toss to coat. Chill overnight. Serves 10 to 12.

potluck pointer

When toting a salad to a get-together, keep it chilled by placing the salad bowl in a larger bowl that is filled with crushed ice.

Mediterranean pasta salad

For variety, substitute shredded Parmesan cheese for the feta cheese and Italian olive oil dressing for the balsamic vinaigrette.

12-oz. pkg. bowtie pasta, cooked
12-oz. jar marinated artichoke
   hearts, drained and chopped
2¼-oz. can sliced black olives,
   drained
1 cucumber, chopped

1 pt. cherry tomatoes
3 T. sweet onion, chopped
8-oz. bottle balsamic vinaigrette
   salad dressing
6-oz. pkg. crumbled feta cheese

Rinse pasta with cold water; drain well. Toss together artichoke hearts and next 5 ingredients with pasta. Chill 2 to 3 hours. Toss with cheese before serving. Serves 8 to 10.

Mary Rose Kulczak
Lambertville, MI

Gooey Caramel Rolls, page 214

bountiful breads

Nothing says home quite like the aroma of freshly baked bread. In this chapter, you will discover the comforts of waking up to quick breads like warm Lemony Apple Muffins (page 210) or Gooey Caramel Rolls (page 214). When dinnertime rolls around, share your bounty with slices of hearty Farmhouse Honey-Wheat Bread (page 227) or cheesy Gruyère Rolls (page 225). And you won't want to miss out on Buttermilk Doughnuts (page 215)...especially the fudgy frosting! So yummy, you'll want to start baking now!

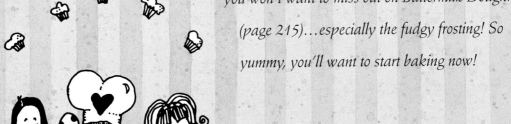

peppery biscuit sticks
(pictured on page 311)

Biscuits or bread sticks…these tasty tidbits are great for dipping in soups, stews and sauces.

2 c. all-purpose flour	¼ t. garlic powder
2 t. baking powder	6 T. chilled butter
¼ t. baking soda	½ c. shredded Parmesan cheese
2 T. sugar	1 egg, beaten
1¼ t. pepper, divided	½ c. plus 2 T. buttermilk, divided

Combine flour, baking powder, baking soda, sugar, ¼ teaspoon pepper and garlic powder in a large bowl. Cut in butter with a pastry blender or 2 forks until mixture resembles coarse crumbs. Stir in cheese. Make a well in center of mixture. Mix egg and ½ cup buttermilk in a small bowl; stir into flour mixture just until moistened.

Turn dough out onto a lightly floured surface; knead just until dough holds together. Pat into a 12"x6" rectangle. Brush lightly with remaining 2 tablespoons buttermilk; sprinkle with remaining one teaspoon pepper and press lightly into dough. Cut into 24 (6-inch-long) strips. Arrange one inch apart on ungreased baking sheets; bake at 450 degrees for 8 minutes or until golden. Makes 2 dozen.

Virginia Watson
Scranton, PA

no time to bake?

Dress up store-bought refrigerated bread sticks in no time. Separate bread stick dough and lay it flat; brush with olive oil and sprinkle sesame seeds and snipped parsley over top. Holding ends of each bread stick, twist 2 times; bake as directed.

fiesta cornbread

(pictured on page 312)

This moist cornbread is chock-full of flavor thanks to creamed corn, onion, sharp Cheddar cheese and 2 jalapeños!

1 c. yellow cornmeal
¾ t. baking soda
½ t. salt
1 c. buttermilk
8¼-oz. can creamed corn
2 eggs, beaten

2 jalapeño peppers, chopped
1 onion, chopped
¼ c. vegetable oil
1½ c. sharp Cheddar cheese,
   shredded and divided

Combine first 3 ingredients in a large bowl. Add buttermilk and next 4 ingredients, stirring just until dry ingredients are moistened.

Heat oil in a 9" cast iron skillet; spoon in half of batter. Sprinkle with one cup cheese; pour remaining batter over top. Sprinkle with remaining ½ cup cheese; bake at 400 degrees for 40 minutes. Serves 6 to 9.

Kathryn Harris
Lufkin, TX

"If you'd like, shred Pepper Jack cheese and substitute it for the Cheddar... it will add more kick!"

Kathryn

strawberry surprise biscuits

Whole strawberries are hidden inside these biscuits, which are sweetened with a powdered sugar glaze.

2 c. all-purpose flour
3 t. baking powder
½ t. salt
2 T. sugar
¼ c. butter

¾ c. plus 1 T. milk, divided
12 strawberries, hulled
⅔ c. powdered sugar
¼ t. vanilla extract

Combine flour, baking powder, salt and sugar in a large bowl. Cut in butter with a pastry blender or 2 forks until mixture is crumbly. Add ¾ cup milk, stirring just until moistened.

Turn dough out onto a lightly floured surface; knead 4 to 5 times. Divide dough into 12 pieces. Pat pieces into 3-inch circles on a floured surface. Place strawberries in centers of circles. Bring dough edges up over strawberries; pinch ends to seal. Place biscuits on a lightly greased baking sheet. Bake at 425 degrees for 18 to 20 minutes or until golden brown.

Stir together powdered sugar, remaining one tablespoon milk and vanilla for glaze. Cool biscuits and drizzle with glaze. Makes one dozen.

Cheri Henry
Newalla, OK

"Take your family to a strawberry farm to pick your own strawberries. What fun!"

Cheri

lemony apple muffins

Lemon zest adds citrusy flavor to these apple muffins. Be sure to scrub the lemon well to remove any wax from the fruit. To zest, rub the fruit against a fine grater or pull a zester across the fruit's rind. You want to remove only the colored skin...not the white pith, which is bitter.

2 c. all-purpose flour	1 c. milk
4 t. baking powder	⅓ c. butter, melted
⅛ t. salt	2 eggs, lightly beaten
½ c. plus 1 T. sugar, divided	zest of one lemon
1 apple, peeled, cored and chopped	1 t. cinnamon

Combine flour, baking powder, salt and ½ cup sugar in a large bowl. Stir in apple and make a well in center of mixture. Combine milk, butter, eggs and lemon zest in a separate bowl; add to flour mixture, stirring just until moistened.

Spoon batter equally into 12 greased muffin cups. Combine remaining one tablespoon sugar and cinnamon; sprinkle over batter. Bake at 425 degrees for 15 minutes or until golden. Cool slightly before removing to a wire rack to cool completely. Makes one dozen.

Vickie
Gooseberry Patch

raspberry scones

(pictured on page 306)

These scones are a nice contribution to breakfast or lunch…or even as a snack! Fresh raspberries are available from May to November, but they can also be purchased frozen or canned.

2 c. all-purpose flour
2½ t. baking powder
¼ t. salt
¼ c. plus 1 T. sugar, divided
⅛ t. ground nutmeg
½ c. chilled butter, sliced

½ c. milk
1 egg, beaten
1 t. lemon zest
¾ c. raspberries
1 T. butter, melted

Combine flour, baking powder, salt, ¼ cup sugar and nutmeg in a large bowl. Cut in chilled butter with a pastry blender or 2 forks until mixture resembles coarse crumbs. Combine milk, egg and lemon zest in a separate bowl; add to dry ingredients, stirring just until moistened. Fold raspberries into dough.

Turn dough out onto a lightly floured surface and knead 8 to 10 times. Place dough in the center of a lightly greased baking sheet. Pat into a 9-inch circle about ½-inch thick. With a sharp knife, cut dough into 8 wedges; do not separate. Brush tops of dough with melted butter and sprinkle with remaining one tablespoon sugar. Bake at 425 degrees for 15 minutes or until golden brown. Cool on a wire rack. Makes 8.

Marlene Darnell
Newport Beach, CA

"These scones are always a hit with overnight guests!"

Marlene

it's tea time!

One of my favorite things to do, whether it's summer or winter, is to have a tea party with friends! During these tea parties, we're all kids again…giggling, sharing secrets and making memories. Scones are one of my favorite breads to serve and share…they always get rave reviews.

Rhonda Whetstone Neibauer
Wisconsin Rapids, WI

peaches & cream French toast

This popular breakfast food is stuffed with a sweet mixture of cream cheese and peach preserves. Don't expect any leftovers…it'll be eaten quickly!

16-oz. loaf French bread, cut into
    8 diagonal slices
8-oz. pkg. cream cheese, softened
⅓ c. peach preserves
3 eggs

½ c. milk
½ t. vanilla extract
¼ t. cinnamon
Optional: powdered sugar,
    maple syrup

Cut a pocket into each bread slice by cutting from the top crust side almost to the bottom crust. (Be careful not to slice completely through bread.) Combine cream cheese and preserves in a small bowl. Spoon mixture evenly into each pocket.

Beat eggs, milk, vanilla and cinnamon in another small bowl until well combined. Dip stuffed bread slices in egg mixture, letting excess drip off. Spray a griddle or skillet with non-stick vegetable spray. Cook bread slices over medium heat until golden brown, about 2 minutes on each side, turning once. Dust each slice with powdered sugar and drizzle with maple syrup, if desired. Serves 4.

Stephanie Moon
Green Bay, WI

"This is absolutely delicious and makes a great breakfast for company!"

Stephanie

gooey caramel rolls
(pictured on page 204)

Three ingredients are all it takes to make up these yummy, gooey breakfast rolls!

1½ c. brown sugar, packed
¾ c. whipping cream

2 loaves frozen bread dough, thawed

Whisk together brown sugar and whipping cream in a small bowl; pour into an ungreased 13"x9" baking pan, coating bottom of pan evenly. Set aside.

Roll out one bread dough loaf into a 12"x6" rectangle; roll up, jelly-roll style, beginning at a short end. Slice into 6 one-inch-thick pieces; arrange in baking pan. Repeat with remaining bread dough loaf. Cover dough; let rise in a warm place (85 degrees) until doubled in bulk.

Uncover and bake at 350 degrees for 35 to 45 minutes; let cool slightly. Invert rolls onto a serving plate. Spoon any remaining syrup on top; serve warm. Makes one dozen.

Maureen Seidl
Inver Grove Heights, MN

midnight breakfast

If you're hosting a sleepover, the kids will likely stay up late giggling. Plan to throw a mini breakfast at midnight! Set up a room filled with games, movies and lots of yummy things to eat...breakfast rolls, muffins and doughnuts.

buttermilk doughnuts

Forget picking up a box of doughnuts at the local store when you can make 4 dozen of your own…plus you get to lick the spoon after you make the fudgy frosting!

2½ c. sugar
2 c. hot mashed potatoes
2 c. buttermilk
2 eggs
6½ to 7 c. all-purpose flour
2 T. butter, melted

2 t. baking soda
2 t. baking powder
½ t. salt
1 t. ground nutmeg
vegetable oil
Frosting

Combine sugar, potatoes, buttermilk and eggs in a large mixing bowl; beat at medium speed with an electric mixer until blended. Combine 6½ cups flour and next 5 ingredients; stir into potato mixture, gradually adding enough remaining flour until a soft dough forms. Turn dough out onto a lightly floured surface and pat to ¾-inch thickness. Using a 2½-inch floured doughnut cutter, cut out dough; repeat procedure with any dough scraps. Pour oil to a depth of one inch in an electric skillet or Dutch oven; heat oil to 375 degrees. Cook doughnuts in batches 2 minutes on each side or until golden brown. Drain on paper towels. Cool on wire racks. Spread Frosting on warm doughnuts. Makes 4 dozen.

frosting:

1 lb. powdered sugar
½ c. baking cocoa
¼ t. salt

⅓ c. boiling water
⅓ c. butter, melted
1 t. vanilla extract

Sift together powdered sugar, cocoa and salt in a bowl; stir in water, butter and vanilla until combined.

Jason Keller
Carrollton, GA

banana-chocolate chip bread

All the toppings of a banana split…bananas, chocolate and cherries…make up the ingredients of this quick loaf bread.

¾ c. butter, softened
1½ c. sugar
3 eggs
3 c. all-purpose flour
1½ t. baking soda

3 bananas, mashed
10-oz. jar maraschino cherries,
    ¼ c. juice reserved
6-oz. pkg. chocolate chips

Beat butter and sugar at medium speed with an electric mixer until creamy. Add eggs, one at a time, beating just until blended after each addition. Combine flour and baking soda; gradually add to butter mixture, beating at low speed just until blended. Stir in mashed bananas, cherries, reserved juice and chocolate chips. Pour into 2 greased 9"x5" loaf pans. Bake at 350 degrees for one hour. Makes 2 loaves.

Bobbi Carney
Aurora, CO

"I like to give this bread as a gift to friends, neighbors and teachers!"

Bobbi

pineapple-zucchini bread

Enjoying your fruits & veggies couldn't be easier! This bread is brimming with zucchini, pineapple, raisins and walnuts.

2 c. sugar
1 c. vegetable oil
3 eggs
3 c. all-purpose flour
2 t. baking soda
1 t. salt
¼ t. baking powder

1½ t. cinnamon
¾ t. ground nutmeg
2 c. zucchini, shredded
8-oz. can crushed pineapple, drained
1 c. raisins
1 c. walnuts, chopped
2 t. vanilla extract

Beat sugar and oil at medium speed with an electric mixer until combined. Add eggs, one at a time, beating just until blended after each addition.

Combine flour, baking soda, salt, baking powder, cinnamon and nutmeg; gradually add to sugar mixture, beating at low speed just until blended. Stir in zucchini, pineapple, raisins, walnuts and vanilla. Pour into 2 greased and floured 9"x5" loaf pans. Bake at 350 degrees for one hour. Makes 2 loaves.

Joyce Wilson
Lonaconing, MD

quick breads

These tasty breads are filled with a bounty of nuts and fruit. For the tenderest loaves and muffins, don't overmix…just stir the batter until moistened. A few lumps won't matter.

cold tea gingerbread

Offer ice cream, lemon sauce or whipped cream with each serving of this gingerbread.

½ c. butter, softened
½ c. sugar
1 egg
1¾ c. all-purpose flour

1 t. baking soda
½ c. cold tea
½ c. molasses

Beat butter and sugar at medium speed with an electric mixer until creamy. Add egg, beating just until blended. Combine flour and baking soda; gradually add to butter mixture, beating at low speed just until blended. Add tea and molasses, beating just until blended. Pour into a greased and floured 9"x5" loaf pan. Bake at 350 degrees for 40 minutes. Makes one loaf.

Michelle Campen
Peoria, IL

"The molasses and tea in this bread make it extra special."

Michelle

apple-Cheddar bread

Apples & Cheddar go together...it's as simple as that!

3 c. all-purpose flour
2 T. baking powder
¾ t. salt
½ c. sugar
1½ c. milk
½ c. vegetable oil

1 egg, beaten
1 egg yolk, beaten
1 small apple, cored, peeled and
    diced
1 c. shredded sharp Cheddar
    cheese

Combine flour, baking powder, salt and sugar in a large mixing bowl.
Combine milk, oil, whole egg and egg yolk in a medium bowl; add to flour
mixture, stirring just until moistened. Gently fold in apple and cheese.

Divide batter between 2 greased 8"x4" loaf pans. Bake at 350 degrees for
about 40 minutes or until a toothpick inserted in center comes out clean. Cool
in pans on a wire rack 10 minutes; remove from pans and cool completely on
wire rack. Store in the refrigerator. Makes 2 loaves.

did you know?

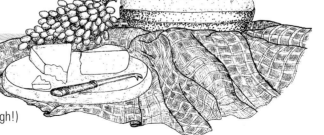

Before the introduction of
coins, the Egyptians gave loaves
of bread as payment for their debts.
(This gives new meaning to the word dough!)

Boston brown bread

This old-fashioned, hearty bread is delicious served warm and spread with butter or cream cheese. It's also the traditional accompaniment for Boston baked beans!

1 c. raisins
1 c. boiling water
1 c. all-purpose flour
1 c. whole-wheat flour
1½ t. baking soda

1 t. salt
1 c. cornmeal
¼ c. brown sugar, packed
2 c. buttermilk
1 c. molasses

Put raisins in a small bowl. Cover with boiling water and let stand 15 minutes.

Combine flours and next 4 ingredients in a large mixing bowl; mix well. Drain raisins and pat dry. Combine buttermilk and molasses in a medium bowl; stir in raisins. Add raisin mixture to flour mixture, stirring just until blended. Pour into a greased 9"x5" loaf pan; bake at 350 degrees for one hour. Makes one loaf.

Regina Vining
Warwick, RI

Cheddar cheese spoonbread

Spoonbread is Southern comfort to the core! This soufflé is baked in a casserole dish and served as a side dish at breakfast, lunch or dinner.

2¼ c. water
1 t. salt
1 c. cornmeal
1 c. milk
1 T. butter

½ t. pepper
4 eggs, beaten
1½ c. shredded sharp
    Cheddar cheese
3 T. scallions, chopped

Bring water to a boil in a large saucepan. Add salt and reduce heat to simmer. Whisk in cornmeal; cook, stirring constantly, about 2 minutes or until mixture is smooth. Remove from heat and whisk in milk, butter and pepper. Whisk in eggs. Stir in cheese and scallions. Pour mixture into a buttered 2-quart baking dish and bake at 400 degrees for 40 minutes or until a toothpick inserted in center comes out clean. Serves 6 to 8.

Gruyère rolls

Yes, these rolls have 3 cups of cheese in them! But the rich, nutty-tasting Gruyère cheese delicately flavors these rolls and does not overpower them.

3 c. all-purpose flour
1 pkg. rapid-rise yeast
3 c. shredded Gruyère cheese
1½ t. salt

¼ t. sugar
1¼ c. water
Optional: melted butter

Combine 2¾ cups flour, yeast and next 3 ingredients in a large mixing bowl. Heat water until very warm (120 to 130 degrees). Gradually add water to flour mixture, beating at high speed with an electric mixer until combined. Beat 2 more minutes at medium speed. Gradually stir in enough remaining flour to make a soft dough.

Turn dough out onto a floured surface and knead until smooth and elastic (about 10 minutes). Place in a well-greased bowl, turning to grease top. Cover and let rise in a warm place (85 degrees), free from drafts, one hour or until doubled in bulk.

Punch dough down; turn out onto a lightly floured surface and knead lightly 4 or 5 times. Divide dough in half. Shape each portion of dough into 8 balls; roll each ball in flour.

Place rolls 2 inches apart on a greased baking sheet. Cover and let rise in a warm place, free from drafts, 30 minutes or until doubled in bulk. Place rolls in oven; spray rolls with water. Bake at 425 degrees for 5 minutes, spraying after 3 minutes without removing rolls from oven. Reduce oven temperature to 350 degrees; continue to bake, without spraying, 13 more minutes or until rolls are golden. Brush with melted butter, if desired. Makes 16 rolls.

brush of herb sprigs

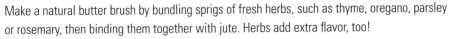

Be sure to place warm melted butter on the table for guests to brush over vegetables or rolls. Make a natural butter brush by bundling sprigs of fresh herbs, such as thyme, oregano, parsley or rosemary, then binding them together with jute. Herbs add extra flavor, too!

lemon fans

For a little variety, try using orange zest instead of lemon zest...for Orange Fans!

¼ c. water
2 pkgs. active dry yeast
2 eggs
1 c. milk
⅓ c. sugar

2 t. lemon zest
1½ t. salt
4 to 4½ c. all-purpose flour
¼ c. butter, melted and divided

Heat water until warm (100 to 110 degrees). Dissolve yeast in warm water in a large bowl; let stand about 5 minutes.

Whisk eggs in a large bowl. Whisk in milk, sugar, lemon zest and salt. Stir in 4 cups flour, ½ cup at a time, until a dough forms. Turn dough out onto a floured surface; knead 6 to 8 minutes or until smooth and elastic, adding more flour, if necessary, to prevent sticking. Place dough in a large, well-greased bowl, turning to grease top. Cover loosely with a damp cloth; let rise in a warm place (85 degrees), free from drafts, 45 minutes to one hour or until doubled in bulk.

Divide dough in half. Roll each half on a lightly floured surface into an 18"x9" rectangle; brush one dough half with one tablespoon butter and cut crosswise into 12 (1½-inch-wide) strips. Then cut lengthwise into 6 (1½-inch-wide) strips, creating 72 squares. Stack 6 squares at a time and place, cut-sides down, in 12 greased muffin cups. Repeat procedure with remaining dough half and one tablespoon butter. Brush tops with remaining 2 tablespoons butter. Cover and let rise in a warm place, free from drafts, until almost doubled in bulk. Bake at 400 degrees for 12 minutes or until golden. Remove from pans and cool completely on wire racks. Makes 2 dozen.

Cindy Watson
Gooseberry Patch

farmhouse honey-wheat bread

This hearty bread is nutritious and delicious, plus it freezes well and makes 2 loaves!

1½ c. water
1 c. small curd cottage cheese
½ c. honey
¼ c. butter
5½ to 6 c. all-purpose flour

1 c. whole-wheat flour
2 T. sugar
3 t. salt
2 pkgs. active dry yeast
1 egg

Heat water, cottage cheese, honey and butter in a saucepan until very warm (about 120 degrees). Combine cottage cheese mixture with 2 cups all-purpose flour, whole-wheat flour and next 4 ingredients in a large mixing bowl; beat at medium speed with an electric mixer 2 minutes. Add enough remaining flour to make a stiff dough. Turn dough out onto a floured surface and knead until smooth and elastic. Place dough in a large, well-greased bowl, turning to grease top; cover and let rise in a warm place (85 degrees), free from drafts, one hour or until doubled in bulk. Punch dough down and shape into 2 loaves; place in 2 greased 9"x5" loaf pans. Cover and let rise 45 minutes or until doubled in bulk. Bake at 350 degrees for 45 minutes or until loaves sound hollow when tapped. Makes 2 loaves.

Mary Murray
Gooseberry Patch

it's done!

To test bread for doneness, thump the crust with your finger. If the loaf sounds hollow, it's done.

braided coffee bread

Every morning is a special occasion when you wake up to the scent of this impressive bread. Surprise your family this weekend!

¼ c. water
1 pkg. active dry yeast
3 T. sugar
½ cup milk, scalded and cooled
4 c. all-purpose flour
3 eggs
½ c. unsalted butter, cut into small pieces

½ t. salt
2 c. sifted powdered sugar
2 T. milk
2 t. vanilla extract
Garnishes: chopped nuts, chopped maraschino cherries

Heat water until warm (100 to 110 degrees). Dissolve yeast in warm water in a large bowl; add sugar. Add milk and ½ cup flour to yeast mixture, beating at medium speed with an electric mixer until smooth. Add eggs, butter and salt, beating until smooth. Stir in remaining 3½ cups flour. Turn dough out onto a well-floured surface; knead dough until smooth and elastic (about 8 minutes). Place in a large, well-greased bowl, turning to grease top.

Cover and let rise in a warm place (85 degrees), free from drafts, one hour and 15 minutes or until doubled in bulk.

Punch dough down and divide into 6 equal portions; form each portion into a 14-inch-long rope. Braid 3 ropes together, tucking in ends. Repeat with remaining 3 ropes. Place braids on a lightly greased baking sheet and let rise in a warm place, free from drafts, one hour or until almost doubled in bulk. Bake at 375 degrees for 20 minutes. Let cool completely.

Combine powdered sugar, milk and vanilla, stirring well; drizzle over loaves. Garnish, if desired. Makes 2 loaves.

Nancy Molldrem
Eau Claire, WI

"I make this coffee bread every Christmas Eve just like my mother did when I was a girl. On Christmas morning, the aroma of fresh-baked bread smells so good."

Nancy

yankee bean pot bread

One of these loaves could be a meal unto itself with such ingredients as bean and bacon soup and shredded wheat biscuits!

6 to 6½ c. all-purpose flour
2 pkgs. active dry yeast
2 T. brown sugar, packed
1 T. salt
1½ c. water
11-oz. can bean and bacon soup, undiluted

2 large shredded wheat biscuits, crumbled
¼ c. molasses
2 T. butter
2 eggs
Optional: melted butter

Combine 2 cups flour, yeast, brown sugar and salt in a large mixing bowl. Combine water, soup, crumbled shredded wheat biscuits, molasses and butter in a saucepan; heat until warm (butter doesn't need to melt). Stir into flour mixture. Add eggs, one at a time, and mix at low speed with an electric mixer until moistened; beat 3 more minutes at medium speed. Gradually stir in enough remaining flour to make a firm dough. Turn dough out onto a floured surface and knead until smooth and elastic (about 5 minutes). Place in a large, well-greased bowl, turning to grease top. Cover and let rise in a warm place (85 degrees), free from drafts, about one hour or until light and doubled in bulk. Punch dough down. Divide into 2 portions. Pat each half into a 14"x7" rectangle on a lightly floured surface. Starting with shorter end, roll up tightly, pressing dough into roll with each turn. Pinch edges and ends to seal. Place in 2 greased 9"x5" loaf pans. Cover and let rise in a warm place, free from drafts, about 45 minutes or until light and doubled in bulk. Bake at 375 degrees for 35 to 40 minutes or until golden brown and loaves sound hollow when tapped. Remove from pans; brush with butter, if desired. Cool. Makes 2 loaves.

Cyndy Rogers
Upton, MA

no sticking!

Spray your measuring cup with non-stick vegetable spray before measuring molasses, syrup or honey. You'll get a more accurate measurement, and the cup will clean up easily!

Greek stuffed bread

Stuffed with spinach, tomatoes, 2 types of cheese and, of course, olives, this tasty bread is best eaten with a fork and knife…you don't want to miss a bite!

10-oz. pkg. frozen chopped spinach, thawed

2⅔ c. water

2 pkgs. active dry yeast

2 t. sugar

6½ c. bread flour

2 t. salt

¾ c. mayonnaise

2 T. dried oregano

1 T. lemon juice

2 t. dried thyme

1 t. dried basil

1 clove garlic, pressed

¾ lb. crumbled feta cheese

1½ c. shredded mozzarella cheese

½ c. tomato, seeded and chopped

1 medium red onion, sliced

20 kalamata olives, pitted and chopped

1 egg, lightly beaten

Cook spinach according to package directions. Drain well and press between paper towels to remove excess moisture. Set aside.

Heat water until warm (100 to 110 degrees). Combine warm water, yeast and sugar in a 4-cup liquid measuring cup; let stand 5 minutes.

Combine yeast mixture, 3¼ cups flour and salt in a large mixing bowl; beat at medium speed with an electric mixer until well blended. Gradually stir in enough of remaining 3¼ cups flour to make a soft dough. Turn dough out onto a well-floured surface and knead until smooth and elastic (about 8 minutes). Place in a well-greased bowl, turning to grease top. Cover and let rise in a warm place (85 degrees), free from drafts, one hour or until doubled in bulk.

Punch dough down; cover and let rest 10 minutes. Turn dough out onto a well-floured surface and knead 4 or 5 times. Roll dough into a 20-inch circle.

Combine mayonnaise and next 5 ingredients. Spread mayonnaise mixture over dough to within ½ inch of edge. Layer cheeses, tomato, onion, olives and spinach over mayonnaise mixture. Fold each side of dough over filling, overlapping edges one inch. Pinch seams to seal. Loaf will be square in shape.

Carefully place loaf, seam-side down, on a greased baking sheet; reshape into a round loaf. Brush with egg. Cut 4 (3-inch-long) slits in top of loaf. Bake at 400 degrees for 35 minutes or until browned. Loaf will be hard but will soften as it cools. Serve warm. Serves 8.

Carrot Cake, page 239

blue-ribbon desserts

Indulge in this yummy collection of made-from-scratch

sweet delights. From Mom's Apple Dumplings (page 235)

to Peanut Butter & Fudge Pie (page 246) to Candy Bar

Fudge (page 271), you'll find that perfect dessert for family

get-togethers, a neighborhood potluck, a

Sunday dinner, or any occasion...

right here. Share these goodies with

family & friends today!

friendship delight

Whip up this easy make-ahead dessert to welcome new neighbors...one bite and your friendship is sealed.

1 c. all-purpose flour
1 c. chopped pecans
½ c. butter, melted
1 c. powdered sugar
12-oz. container frozen whipped topping, thawed and divided

8-oz. pkg. cream cheese
4 c. milk, divided
4-oz. pkg. chocolate instant pudding
4-oz. pkg. vanilla instant pudding
Garnish: additional chopped nuts

Combine first 3 ingredients in a small bowl and press evenly into a 13"x9" pan. Bake at 325 degrees for 25 minutes or until lightly browned.

Beat powdered sugar and half of whipped topping at medium speed with an electric blender until combined; beat in cream cheese until combined. Spread over cooled crust.

Mix 2 cups milk with each pudding mix. Layer chocolate pudding over cream cheese layer; spread to edges. Layer vanilla pudding over chocolate pudding and top with remaining half of whipped topping. Sprinkle with additional chopped nuts, if desired. Refrigerate 3 to 4 hours before serving. Serves 10 to 12.

Lisa Engelhardt
Tavernier, FL

birthday cake

A family favorite was always my mama's birthday pound cake. Back then, before stand mixers, this cake was a two-person job! One of us would beat the eggs, while the other gathered all the other ingredients. We always used a big, green Fire-King bowl to mix the cake in and, later on, Mama gave it to me...I treasure it. Served frosted or with fruit or ice cream, this cake has been loved by four generations of our family over the last 40 years.

Rhonda Jones
Rocky Mount, VA

Mom's apple dumplings

This classic apple dessert is wrapped in homemade pastry, sprinkled with cinnamon-nutmeg-sugar mixture and topped with cinnamon syrup.

1½ c. sugar

1½ c. water

¼ t. cinnamon

¼ t. ground nutmeg

8 drops red food coloring

3 T. butter

2 c. all-purpose flour

2 t. baking powder

1 t. salt

⅔ c. shortening

½ c. milk

6 apples

additional sugar, cinnamon,
    ground nutmeg

6 T. butter

Prepare syrup by combining sugar, water, cinnamon, nutmeg and food coloring in a saucepan; bring to a boil. Remove from heat and add 3 tablespoons butter; set aside.

Combine flour, baking powder and salt; cut in shortening with a pastry blender or 2 forks until mixture is crumbly. Gradually add milk, stirring with a fork until dry ingredients are moistened. Shape mixture into a ball; roll pastry on a lightly floured surface, shaping into an 18"x12" rectangle.

Peel and core apples. Cut pastry into 6 (6-inch) squares and place an apple on each square. Sprinkle generously with additional sugar, cinnamon and nutmeg; dot each apple with one tablespoon butter. Moisten edges of each pastry square with water; bring corners to center, pressing edges to seal. Place in an ungreased pan and pour syrup over dumplings. Bake at 375 degrees for 35 minutes. Serves 6.

Sharon Gibbons
Knoxville, TN

"These apple dumplings always remind me of growing up and the happiness of home."

Sharon

ice-cream tacos

The next time you want tacos, make them the dessert kind! These sweet treats are stuffed with ice cream, drizzled with hot fudge and finished with a cherry on top.

8 frozen round waffles, thawed
1 qt. chocolate ice cream, softened
½ c. mini marshmallows

½ c. hot fudge sauce, warmed
8 maraschino cherries with stems

Warm waffles; do not toast. Gently fold each waffle in half; set in a 13"x9" baking dish, open-side up, keeping the rows tight so taco shape is maintained.

Combine ice cream and marshmallows in a large mixing bowl; spoon evenly into waffle shells. Cover and freeze until firm. Before serving, drizzle with warmed hot fudge sauce and top each with a cherry. Serves 8.

Kathy Unruh
Fresno, CA

"The kids will love these...they're so fun to eat!"

Kathy

double trouble

Chocolate frosting coats this two-layer chocolate cake, giving the lucky recipients double trouble…of the chocolate-indulgence kind!

1¾ c. all-purpose flour
1½ t. baking soda
½ t. salt
½ c. butter, softened
¾ c. brown sugar, packed
⅔ c. sugar
2 eggs

1½ t. vanilla extract
½ c. sour cream
4 (1-oz.) squares unsweetened
   baking chocolate, melted and
   cooled
1 c. buttermilk
Frosting

Combine flour, baking soda and salt in a small bowl; set aside. Beat butter in a large bowl at medium speed with an electric mixer until creamy. Add sugars and beat one minute. Add eggs, one at a time, beating well after each addition; stir in vanilla. Add sour cream; beat 30 seconds. Stir in melted chocolate, mixing well. Add flour mixture to chocolate mixture alternately with buttermilk, beginning and ending with flour mixture; beat well.

Pour batter into 2 greased and floured 8" round cake pans. Bake at 350 degrees for 25 to 35 minutes or until a toothpick inserted in center comes out clean. Cool in pans on a wire rack 10 minutes; remove from pans and cool completely on wire rack.

Spread Frosting between layers and on top and sides of cake. Serves 12.

frosting:

14-oz. can sweetened condensed
   milk
½ c. butter

3 (1-oz.) squares unsweetened
   baking chocolate
2 t. vanilla extract

Heat milk, butter and chocolate in a saucepan over low heat, stirring constantly, until butter and chocolate melt and frosting thickens, about 3 minutes. Remove from heat; stir in vanilla. Let cool 5 minutes before frosting cooled cake.

Jennifer Licon-Conner
Gooseberry Patch

carrot cake

(pictured on page 232)

Crushed pineapple adds extra moistness to this scrumptious carrot cake.

3 c. all-purpose flour
2 t. baking powder
2 t. baking soda
1 t. salt
2 t. cinnamon
4 eggs
2½ c. sugar

1½ c. vegetable oil
1 t. vanilla extract
2 large carrots, grated
15¼-oz. can crushed pineapple,
   drained
1½ c. chopped nuts
Frosting

Stir together first 5 ingredients in a medium bowl. Beat eggs and next 3 ingredients in a large mixing bowl at medium speed with an electric mixer until smooth. Add flour mixture, beating at low speed until blended. Fold in carrots, pineapple and nuts.

Pour batter into 3 greased and floured 9" round cake pans. Bake at 350 degrees for 25 to 30 minutes or until a toothpick inserted in center comes out clean. Cool in pans on wire racks 10 minutes. Remove from pans and cool completely on wire racks. Spread Frosting between layers and on top and sides of cake. Serves 16.

frosting:

2 (8-oz.) pkgs. cream cheese,
   softened
½ c. butter
2 (16-oz.) pkgs. powdered sugar,
   sifted

2 t. vanilla extract
1 c. chopped nuts

Beat cream cheese and butter at medium speed with an electric mixer until smooth. Gradually add powdered sugar, beating at low speed until light and fluffy. Stir in vanilla and nuts. Makes 6¾ cups.

Karen Moran
Navasota, TX

"I remember my mother baking this for my father's birthday...it was his favorite cake!"

Karen

buttery pound cake

The sweet brown sugar glaze pairs perfectly with the apples!

½ c. plus ⅓ c. brown sugar, packed and divided

⅓ c. chopped pecans, toasted

1 t. cinnamon

1 t. ground nutmeg

¾ c. plus 2 T. butter, softened and divided

1½ c. sugar

3 eggs

3 c. all-purpose flour

1½ t. baking powder

1½ t. baking soda

½ t. salt

1½ c. sour cream

2 t. vanilla extract, divided

1½ c. apple, peeled, cored and thinly sliced

2 T. milk

Combine ⅓ cup brown sugar, pecans, cinnamon and nutmeg in a small bowl; set aside.

Beat ¾ cup butter at medium speed with an electric mixer until creamy. Gradually add 1½ cups sugar, beating 5 to 7 minutes. Add eggs, one at a time, beating just until yellow disappears.

Combine flour, baking powder, baking soda and salt in another bowl. Add sour cream and flour mixture alternately to butter mixture, beginning and ending with flour mixture; beat at low speed after each addition just until mixture is blended. Stir in one teaspoon vanilla.

Spoon half of batter into a greased and floured 12-cup Bundt® pan. Arrange apple slices over batter, then spoon half of brown sugar mixture over apples; gently press into batter. Top with remaining batter, then sprinkle with remaining brown sugar mixture. Bake at 350 degrees for one hour or until a toothpick inserted in center comes out clean. Cool in pan on a wire rack 15 minutes; remove from pan and cool completely on wire rack.

Heat 2 tablespoons butter in a small saucepan over medium heat until butter starts to brown. Remove from heat and stir in remaining ½ cup brown sugar, milk and one teaspoon vanilla. Stir until smooth; drizzle glaze evenly over cake. Serves 16.

Cheryl Bierley
Miamisburg, OH

white Texas sheet cake

A nice change from the chocolate version...and just as delicious!

1 c. butter	2 c. sugar
1 c. water	2 eggs, beaten
2 c. all-purpose flour	½ c. sour cream
1 t. baking soda	1 t. almond extract
1 t. salt	Frosting

Bring butter and water to a boil in a large saucepan. Remove from heat and whisk in flour, baking soda, salt, sugar, eggs, sour cream and almond extract until smooth. Pour into a greased 15"x10" baking pan. Bake at 375 degrees for 20 to 22 minutes or until a toothpick inserted in center comes out clean. Cool in pan on a wire rack 20 minutes. Spread Frosting on top of cake. Serves 12.

frosting:

½ c. butter	½ t. almond extract
¼ c. milk	1 c. chopped walnuts
4½ c. powdered sugar	

Combine butter and milk in a saucepan; cook over low heat until butter melts. Bring to a boil over medium heat.

Remove from heat and add powdered sugar and almond extract; beat at medium speed with an electric mixer until spreading consistency. Stir in walnuts.

Sandra Warren
Friendship, OH

red velvet cake

(pictured on page 309)

This cake makes a stunning appearance with its reddish cake layers and white frosting…perfect for any festive occasion.

½ c. shortening	1 t. baking soda
1½ c. sugar	¾ t. salt
2 eggs	3 T. baking cocoa
1 t. vanilla extract	1 c. buttermilk
1½ T. red food coloring	1 T. white vinegar
2 c. all-purpose flour	Best-Ever Soft Icing

Beat shortening and sugar at medium speed with an electric mixer until fluffy. Add eggs, one at a time, beating just until yellow disappears. Stir in vanilla and food coloring.

Combine flour, baking soda, salt and cocoa. Stir together buttermilk and vinegar; add to shortening mixture alternately with flour mixture, beginning and ending with flour mixture. Beat just until blended after each addition. Pour batter into 2 greased and floured 9" round cake pans; bake at 350 degrees for 25 minutes or until a toothpick inserted in center comes out clean. Cool in pans on a wire rack 10 minutes; remove from pans. Cool completely on wire racks. Spread Best-Ever Soft Icing between layers and on top and sides of cake. Serves 12.

best-ever soft icing:

¼ c. all-purpose flour	1 t. vanilla extract
1 c. milk	1 c. sugar
1 c. butter, softened	

Whisk together flour and milk in a small saucepan over low heat until thickened. Pour into a mixing bowl; allow mixture to cool. Add butter and remaining ingredients to flour mixture; beat at high speed with an electric mixer until fluffy, about 8 minutes. Makes 3½ cups.

Marion Pfeifer
Smyrna, DE

"I've found that the men in our family just love this cake! It's always requested for birthdays, graduations or any special gathering."

Marion

ice-cream cone cakes

Surprise the birthday honoree with cake made in ice-cream cones. Everything is edible, and there are no forks & plates to clean up!

⅔ c. all-purpose flour
1 t. baking powder
⅛ t. salt
⅓ c. baking cocoa
2 T. butter, softened
½ c. sugar
⅔ c. buttermilk

½ t. vanilla extract
1 egg white
10 flat-bottomed ice-cream cones
Frosting
Optional: colored sprinkles,
     10 maraschino cherries with
     stems

Combine first 4 ingredients in a small bowl; set aside.

Beat butter and sugar in a large mixing bowl at medium speed with an electric mixer until creamy. Add flour mixture and buttermilk alternately to butter mixture, beginning and ending with flour mixture; beat at low speed after each addition just until blended. Stir in vanilla. Add egg white, mixing well.

Fill cones to within ½ inch of the top; carefully place on an ungreased baking sheet. Bake at 375 degrees for 35 minutes; cool completely on wire racks. Spread evenly with Frosting. Top with colored sprinkles and a cherry, if desired. Serves 10.

frosting:

2 T. butter, softened
1½ c. powdered sugar

2 T. buttermilk
1½ t. vanilla extract

Beat butter and sugar at medium speed with an electric mixer until creamy. Add buttermilk; beat until spreading consistency. Stir in vanilla. Makes about ⅔ cup.

Kris Lammers
Gooseberry Patch

"Ice-cream cones that don't melt...my family loves 'em!"

Kris

peanut butter & fudge pie

This pie is like an ice-cream sundae...full of the same toppings but with a hint of peanut butter.

½ c. creamy peanut butter
¼ c. honey
1 qt. vanilla ice cream, softened
9-oz. graham cracker pie crust
½ c. cashews, chopped
½ c. fudge ice-cream topping,
     warmed

Garnishes: whipped topping,
     additional warmed fudge
     ice-cream topping and chopped
     cashews

Combine peanut butter and honey; stir in ice cream. Spoon half of ice-cream mixture into pie crust; sprinkle with half of cashews. Drizzle half of fudge ice-cream topping over cashews; spoon remaining ice-cream mixture over top. Sprinkle with remaining cashews and drizzle with remaining fudge ice-cream topping. Freeze about 8 hours or until firm. Garnish with whipped topping, additional warmed fudge ice-cream topping and chopped cashews, if desired. Serves 8.

Coli Harrington
Delaware, OH

honey-crunch pecan pie

A splash of bourbon and a measure of golden honey add to this impressive nut-filled dessert. Chopped pecans flavor the filling, while glazed pecan halves crown the surface.

4 eggs, lightly beaten
1 c. light corn syrup
¼ c. sugar
¼ c. brown sugar, packed
2 T. butter, melted
1 T. bourbon
1 t. vanilla extract

½ t. salt
1 c. chopped pecans
10-inch unbaked pie crust
¼ c. plus 3 T. brown sugar, packed
¼ c. butter
⅓ c. honey
2 c. pecan halves

Combine first 8 ingredients in a large bowl; stir well with a wire whisk until blended. Stir in chopped pecans. Spoon pecan mixture into pie crust. Bake at 350 degrees for 35 minutes. Cover with aluminum foil after 25 minutes to prevent excessive browning, if necessary.

Meanwhile, combine ¼ cup plus 3 tablespoons brown sugar, ¼ cup butter and honey in a medium saucepan; cook over medium heat 2 minutes or until sugar dissolves and butter melts, stirring often. Add pecan halves and stir gently until coated. Spoon pecan mixture evenly over pie. Bake 10 more minutes or until topping is bubbly. Cool completely on a wire rack. Serves 10.

mile-high lemon meringue pie

This lemon pie is piled high with a layer of billowy meringue.

½ (15-oz.) pkg. refrigerated pie crust
8-oz. container sour cream
5 eggs, separated
2.9-oz. pkg. cook-and-serve lemon
    pudding mix
1 c. milk

½ c. plus 2 T. lemonade concentrate,
    thawed
¼ t. cream of tartar
½ t. vanilla extract
½ c. plus 2 T. sugar

Unroll pie crust according to package directions. Fit into a 9" pie plate. Fold edges under and flute. Prick bottom and sides with a fork. Bake at 450 degrees until golden. Remove from oven and let cool on a wire rack. Reduce oven temperature to 350 degrees.

Whisk together sour cream and egg yolks in a medium saucepan; stir in lemon pudding mix, milk and lemonade concentrate. Cook over medium heat, whisking constantly, until thickened. Reduce heat to low and cook 2 minutes or until very thick. Remove from heat; cover and keep hot.

Beat egg whites, cream of tartar and vanilla at high speed with an electric mixer until foamy. Beat in sugar, one tablespoon at a time, until stiff peaks form. Pour hot filling into prepared crust. Dollop meringue onto hot filling. Lightly spread dollops together in decorative swirls, completely sealing meringue to pie crust. Bake at 325 degrees for 22 to 25 minutes or until golden. Cool completely on a wire rack. Serves 8.

Scott Harrington
Boston, MA

chocolate Sunday pie

Make any day of the week exceptional when you offer this thick & rich chocolatey pie for dessert.

1½ c. sugar	1 T. butter
¼ c. all-purpose flour	1 t. vanilla extract
5 T. baking cocoa	9-inch pie crust, baked
2 c. milk	Meringue
3 egg yolks, lightly beaten	

Combine sugar, flour and cocoa in a medium saucepan. Gradually add milk, stirring well. Gradually add egg yolks to chocolate mixture; add butter. Cook mixture over medium heat about 20 minutes or until thickened, stirring often. Remove from heat and stir in vanilla. Pour into pie crust and dollop Meringue onto hot pie filling. Lightly spread dollops together in decorative swirls, completely sealing Meringue to pie crust. Bake at 350 degrees for 10 minutes or until Meringue is golden. Cool completely on a wire rack. Serves 8.

meringue:

3 egg whites	¼ c. sugar
¼ t. cream of tartar	

Beat egg whites and cream of tartar at high speed with an electric mixer until foamy. Beat in sugar, one tablespoon at a time, until stiff peaks form.

Sandra Crook
Jacksonville, FL

blackberry cobbler

Use fresh blackberries when they're at their peak during May and June. And if time allows, churn some homemade vanilla ice cream to top off this ultimate comfort food!

1 c. butter, divided
1 c. plus 2 T. sugar, divided
1 c. water
1½ c. self-rising flour

⅓ c. milk, room temperature
2 c. fresh or frozen blackberries
1 t. cinnamon

Melt ½ cup butter in a 10" round or oval baking dish; set aside.

Heat one cup sugar and water in a saucepan until sugar dissolves; set aside. Place flour in a large mixing bowl and cut in remaining ½ cup butter with a pastry blender or 2 forks until mixture is crumbly. Add milk and stir with a fork to form a dough. Continue stirring until dough leaves the sides of the bowl.

Turn out dough onto a lightly floured surface; knead 3 or 4 times and roll to ¼-inch thickness, shaping into an 11"x9" rectangle. Sprinkle berries over dough; sprinkle with cinnamon and roll up, jelly-roll style. Cut into ¼-inch-thick slices and carefully place slices in baking dish over melted butter. Pour sugar syrup around slices. Bake at 350 degrees for 45 minutes. Sprinkle remaining 2 tablespoons sugar over top and bake 15 more minutes. Serve warm or cold. Serves 8.

Pat Habiger
Spearville, KS

"My grandmother made this cobbler when I was a little girl. I would play on Grandpa and Grandma's farm, which had a large garden, a goldfish tank and a tree swing that would almost touch the sky! Grandma would crochet, quilt and make the greatest desserts."

Pat

glazed strawberry tart

Really show off this tart on special occasions…drizzle it with melted chocolate or dust it with powdered sugar!

1½ c. all-purpose flour
½ c. almonds, ground
⅓ c. sugar
½ t. salt
6 T. chilled butter, sliced
1 egg
1 t. almond extract

¾ c. strawberry jam
1 t. lemon juice
2 pts. strawberries, hulled and
　　halved
Optional: whipped topping
Garnish: whole strawberry

Combine flour, almonds, sugar and salt in a large mixing bowl; cut in butter with a pastry blender or 2 forks until mixture is crumbly. Whisk together egg and almond extract in another bowl; add to flour mixture, stirring until a dough forms. Shape into a flattened ball; wrap in plastic wrap and refrigerate overnight.

Place dough in center of a greased and floured baking sheet. Pat into a 10-inch circle; form a ¾-inch-high rim around the outside edge. Prick bottom of dough with a fork; bake at 350 degrees for 25 minutes or until golden. Cool 10 minutes on baking sheet on a wire rack; remove crust from baking sheet and cool completely on wire rack.

Heat jam and lemon juice in a small saucepan over low heat until spreadable; spread ½ cup jam mixture over crust. Arrange berry halves on top, cut-sides down; brush with remaining jam mixture. Serve with whipped topping and garnish, if desired. Serves 8.

Jo Ann
Gooseberry Patch

vintage finds

Look for vintage pie tins, servers and cake plates at flea markets…add them to your collection or make them part of the gift when sharing a favorite sweet treat.

baby cakes

Use your favorite shaped cookie cutter or a variety of shapes to make these creamy butter cookies.

2 c. all-purpose flour
1 c. butter, softened
⅓ c. whipping cream

sugar to taste
Creamy Filling

Beat flour, butter and cream at medium speed with an electric mixer until combined; chill one hour.

Roll dough to an ⅛- to ¼-inch thickness on a lightly floured surface. Cut with tiny cookie cutters; place close together on ungreased baking sheets. Pierce each cookie several times with a fork; sprinkle lightly with sugar. Bake at 375 degrees for about 8 minutes or until golden. Remove to wire racks to cool completely. Spread Creamy Filling between cookies, forming sandwiches. Makes about 4½ dozen.

creamy filling:

¼ c. butter, softened
¾ c. powdered sugar

1 t. vanilla extract

Beat butter at medium speed with an electric mixer until creamy; gradually add sugar, beating well. Stir in vanilla.

Renée Spec
Crescent, PA

brown sugar cookies

A hint of maple syrup makes these cookies appealing!

2⅓ c. brown sugar, packed
1 c. butter, softened
2 eggs

1 t. vanilla extract
½ t. maple syrup
2 c. all-purpose flour

Beat first 5 ingredients at medium speed with an electric mixer until well blended. Gradually add flour, mixing well. Drop dough by tablespoonfuls onto ungreased baking sheets. Bake at 375 degrees for 8 minutes. Remove to wire racks to cool. Makes 3 dozen.

Lisa Watkins
Gooseberry Patch

storage containers

Search flea markets, yard sales or antique shops for unique biscuit or pickle jars and old-style bottles. They're just right to fill with sweet treats for friends or to set on your counter filled with after-school snacks!

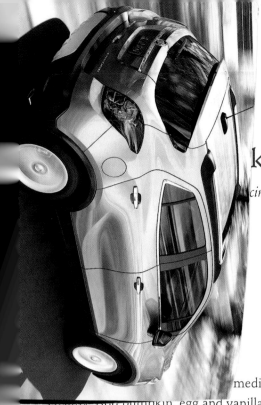

kin cookies

...cinnamon, these cookies will make you...

1 t. baking soda
½ t. salt
1 t. cinnamon
1 c. semi-sweet chocolate chips
Frosting

...medium speed with an electric mixer until creamy. Add pumpkin, egg and vanilla, beating until blended; set aside.

Combine flour, baking soda, salt and cinnamon in a small bowl; gradually add to shortening mixture, beating well. Fold in chocolate chips.

Drop by tablespoonfuls onto ungreased baking sheets. Bake at 350 degrees for 15 to 20 minutes or until golden and browned on bottom. Remove to wire racks to cool. Drizzle cookies with Frosting. Makes 2 dozen.

frosting:

½ c. brown sugar, packed
3 T. butter

3 T. milk
1½ c. powdered sugar

Combine brown sugar, butter and milk in a small saucepan. Bring mixture to a boil over medium heat; boil 2 minutes. Remove from heat. Add powdered sugar. Beat at medium speed with an electric mixer until mixture is smooth.

Susan Whitney
Fountain Valley, CA

lunch-box surprise

Surprise 'em at lunch by slipping cookies inside vellum envelopes and tying them closed with shoestring licorice!

sugared pecan cookies

These log-shaped cookies are just perfect when dipped in a tall, cold glass of milk!

½ c. butter, softened
½ c. cream cheese, softened
1 t. vanilla extract
1¾ c. all-purpose flour

1 T. sugar
⅛ t. salt
1 c. pecan halves, ground
1 c. powdered sugar

Beat butter and cream cheese at medium speed with an electric mixer until creamy. Stir in vanilla and set aside.

Combine flour, one tablespoon sugar and salt; gradually add to butter mixture, beating well. Stir in pecans. Shape each tablespoonful of dough into a 2-inch log. Place 2 inches apart on ungreased baking sheets; bake at 375 degrees for 12 to 14 minutes. Roll warm cookies in powdered sugar; cool on wire racks. Makes 2 dozen.

Kathy McLaren
Visalia, CA

frosted orange cookies

These light-tasting, citrus-flavored cookies are eye-catching at baby or wedding showers.

1 c. shortening

1½ c. sugar

2 eggs

1 T. orange zest

⅓ c. orange juice

4 c. all-purpose flour

4 t. baking powder

1 t. baking soda

⅛ t. salt

1 c. milk

1 T. lemon juice

Frosting

Beat shortening and sugar at medium speed with an electric mixer until creamy; add eggs, beating until blended. Add zest and orange juice, beating until combined. Combine flour, baking powder, baking soda and salt. Stir together milk and lemon juice; add to shortening mixture alternately with flour mixture, beginning and ending with flour mixture. Drop by tablespoonfuls onto parchment paper-lined baking sheets; bake at 350 degrees for 9 to 10 minutes. Remove to wire racks. Spread with Frosting while still warm. Makes about 4 dozen.

frosting:

1-lb. pkg. powdered sugar

1 T. orange zest

4 to 5 T. orange juice

Beat sugar, one tablespoon orange zest and 4 tablespoons orange juice at medium speed with an electric mixer until creamy; add enough remaining orange juice to reach desired spreading consistency.

Laura Lett
Gooseberry Patch

white chocolate-cranberry cookies

Dried cranberries taste surprisingly sweet. When paired with white chocolate, they'll make these cookies a favorite choice.

½ c. butter, softened
¾ c. sugar
½ c. brown sugar, packed
1 egg, beaten
1 t. vanilla extract

1¾ c. all-purpose flour
1 t. baking powder
½ t. baking soda
1 c. sweetened dried cranberries
½ c. white chocolate chips

Beat butter in a large bowl at medium speed with an electric mixer until creamy; gradually add sugars, beating until combined. Add egg and vanilla; beat until smooth.

Combine flour, baking powder and baking soda; gradually add to sugar mixture, beating well. Stir in cranberries and chocolate chips.

Shape dough into 1½-inch balls; place 2 inches apart on ungreased baking sheets. Bake at 375 degrees for 14 minutes or until golden. Remove to wire racks to cool. Makes about 2½ dozen.

Shawna Brock
Eglin AFB, FL

peanut butter jumbos

*These cookies are big on flavor. They're loaded with peanut butter, oats,
chocolate chips and chocolate candy!*

¼ c. butter, softened
1 c. brown sugar, packed
1 c. sugar
1½ c. creamy peanut butter
3 eggs
1 t. vanilla extract

4½ c. quick-cooking oats,
   uncooked
2 t. baking soda
1 c. chocolate chips
1 c. candy-coated chocolate
   mini-baking bits

Beat butter, sugars and peanut butter at medium speed with an electric
mixer until creamy. Add eggs and vanilla, beating until blended. Combine
oats and baking soda; add to butter mixture, beating just until blended. Fold in
chocolate chips and mini-baking bits.

Drop by tablespoonfuls onto greased baking sheets. Bake at 350 degrees
for 15 to 20 minutes. Remove to wire racks to cool. Makes about 1½ dozen.

Julie Anthony
Homeworth, OH

decorating tip

Add chocolate or peanut butter chips
to a plastic zipping bag and microwave until
the chips are melted. Then just snip off
one small corner of the bag and pipe
designs onto the cooled cookies.

ice box brownies

These chewy brownies are almost like eating fudge…wonderful!

¼ c. butter
1½ squares unsweetened chocolate
1 c. brown sugar, packed
1 egg, beaten
½ c. all-purpose flour
¼ t. baking powder
¼ t. salt
¼ t. vanilla extract
½ c. chopped walnuts
Mint Filling
Glaze

Microwave butter and chocolate in a one-quart glass bowl on high for one minute or until melted. Add sugar and egg, stirring until blended. Combine flour, baking powder and salt; stir into chocolate mixture. Stir in vanilla and walnuts. Pour into a greased 8"x8" pan and bake at 350 degrees for 15 to 18 minutes. Remove from oven and cool completely on a wire rack.

Spread Mint Filling over brownies. Chill 30 minutes. Spread Glaze over filling. Cut into squares to serve and store brownies in the refrigerator. Makes 16.

mint filling:

2 c. powdered sugar
¼ c. butter, softened
2 T. milk
¾ t. peppermint extract
½ t. vanilla extract
few drops green food coloring

Beat all ingredients at medium speed with an electric mixer 2 to 3 minutes or until smooth. Chill about 30 minutes.

glaze:

2 squares unsweetened chocolate   1 T. butter

Melt chocolate and butter in a small saucepan over low heat, stirring until smooth.

Tami Bowman
Gooseberry Patch

cream cheese bar cookies

Coconut is a flavorful surprise in these creamy bar cookies!

2¼ c. all-purpose flour, divided
1 c. butter, softened
½ c. sugar
½ c. cornstarch
4 eggs
16-oz. pkg. brown sugar

½ t. baking powder
2 t. vanilla extract
½ c. chopped walnuts
½ c. sweetened flaked coconut
Cream Cheese Topping

Combine 2 cups flour, butter, ½ cup sugar and cornstarch with a pastry blender or 2 forks until mixture resembles fine crumbs. Press mixture evenly into an ungreased jelly-roll pan; bake at 350 degrees for 18 minutes.

Beat eggs, brown sugar, remaining ¼ cup flour, baking powder and vanilla at medium speed with an electric mixer until blended; stir in walnuts and coconut. Spread on top of crust.

Bake at 350 degrees for 10 minutes. Let cool in pan on a wire rack; spread with Cream Cheese Topping and bake 30 more minutes or until set. Cut into bars. Makes 3½ to 4 dozen.

cream cheese topping:

8-oz. pkg. cream cheese, softened
½ c. butter, softened

1 t. vanilla extract
16-oz. pkg. powdered sugar

Beat first 3 ingredients at medium speed with an electric mixer until creamy; gradually add sugar, beating until blended. Makes 3½ cups.

Amy Prather
Longview, WA

"My mother-in-law always made these delicious cookies... now I'm carrying on the tradition."

Amy

lemon-oatmeal bars

The zest of two fruits adds extra flavor to these oatmeal bars. Zest each fruit before juicing it by pulling a zester across or down the fruit's rind or by rubbing the fruit against a fine grater. Only remove each fruit's colored skin, not the bitter white part.

1 c. butter, softened
1 c. sugar
2 c. all-purpose flour
1¼ c. long-cooking oats, uncooked

zest and juice of 2 lemons
zest and juice of 1 orange
14-oz. can sweetened condensed milk

Beat butter and sugar at medium speed with an electric mixer until creamy. Add flour and oats, stirring to make a crumbly dough. Press two-thirds of dough into a greased 13"x9" baking pan; set aside. Stir zests and juices into condensed milk; spread evenly over dough in pan. Sprinkle remaining dough over top. Bake at 350 degrees for 30 to 35 minutes or until golden. Cool completely on a wire rack; cut into squares to serve. Makes 2½ to 3 dozen.

Carrie Kiiskila
Racine, WI

recipe place card

Here's a cookie swap table tent with a holiday feel...jot each cookie's name on a piece of cardstock, then tuck each card into a pinecone.

Aunt Mary's praline pecans

*Aunt Mary had the right idea when she passed down this recipe for quick
& easy pralines...they're made in the microwave!*

2 c. sugar
1 c. brown sugar, packed
1 c. evaporated milk
2 c. chopped pecans

2 T. butter
1 t. vanilla extract
⅛ t. salt

Combine sugars and evaporated milk in a 4-quart microwave-safe
glass measuring cup. Microwave on high for 6 minutes; stir well. Add nuts,
butter, vanilla and salt; microwave on high 6 more minutes. Stir until thickened. Working rapidly, drop by heaping teaspoonfuls onto wax paper; let cool.
Makes about 3 dozen.

Sandy White
Elmer, LA

rocky road-peanut butter candy cups

"Rocky road" gets its name from the combination of chocolate, miniature marshmallows and nuts.

11-oz. pkg. peanut butter and milk
    chocolate chips
2 T. creamy peanut butter
1 c. crispy rice cereal

1 c. miniature marshmallows
¾ c. unsalted roasted peanuts,
    chopped

Microwave peanut butter and milk chocolate chips in a large glass bowl on high for one to 2 minutes or until melted, stirring every 30 seconds. Stir in peanut butter until well blended.

Stir in rice cereal, miniature marshmallows and chopped peanuts. Spoon mixture by heaping tablespoonfuls evenly into miniature paper candy cups. Chill one hour or until firm. Makes about 3 dozen.

Copy & attach!

Nothing's Better Than home♥made

♥...something sweet... ♥...a bake sale treat♥

cola candy

Substitute your favorite dark soft drink in the candy and frosting.

3½ c. vanilla wafer crumbs

2 c. powdered sugar

1 c. chopped pecans

½ c. cola

2 T. butter, melted

Cola Frosting

Stir together first 5 ingredients; shape mixture into one-inch balls. Cover and chill at least 30 minutes.

Dip balls in Cola Frosting; chill until ready to serve. Makes 2 dozen.

cola frosting:

¾ c. powdered sugar

⅓ c. cola

¼ c. butter, softened

¼ t. vanilla extract

Stir together all ingredients in a small bowl. Makes one cup.

candy bar fudge

Caramels, peanuts and chocolate make up this candylike fudge.

½ c. butter, softened
⅓ c. baking cocoa
¼ c. brown sugar, packed
¼ c. milk
2½ c. powdered sugar
1 t. vanilla extract

30 caramel candies, unwrapped
2 T. water
2 c. unsalted peanuts
½ c. semi-sweet chocolate chips
½ c. milk chocolate chips

Combine first 4 ingredients in a microwave-safe bowl; microwave on high for 3 minutes or until mixture boils, stirring after one minute. Stir in powdered sugar and vanilla; pour into a buttered 8"x8" baking dish and set aside.

Heat caramels and water in another microwave-safe bowl on high 2 minutes or until melted, stirring after one minute; stir in peanuts. Spread over chocolate mixture; set aside.

Microwave chocolate chips in a microwave-safe bowl on high one minute, stirring until melted. Pour evenly over caramel layer. Refrigerate until firm. Cut into squares. Makes 2½ pounds.

Susan Brzozowski
Ellicott City, MD

"This fudge is more like a candy bar...everyone loves it!"

Susan

chocolate cutouts

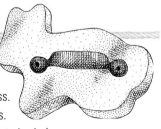

Mini cookie cutters are just the right size to make chocolate cutouts. Pour melted semi-sweet chocolate onto wax paper-lined cookie sheets and spread to ⅛-inch thickness. Refrigerate until firm and then cut shapes with cookie cutters. Remove from wax paper and chill...a sweet garnish on a frosted cake!

Master Cookie Mix, page 303

gifts
from the kitchen

There's always a reason for giving, and the best gifts come from the heart or, in our case…the kitchen! For your next gift-giving occasion, tie up bags of Angie's Chai Tea Mix (page 274), can some fresh Pear Honey (page 281) or whip up some White Chocolate Fudge (page 302). These and our other selections of homemade treats will be welcomed by all!

Angie's chai tea mix

This Indian tea is quickly becoming popular throughout our country. Keep this mix on hand to stir up for soothing moments during your day.

2½ c. powdered sugar
1 c. instant tea mix
1 c. powdered milk
1 c. powdered non-dairy creamer
½ c. vanilla-flavored powdered non-dairy creamer

1½ t. pumpkin pie spice
½ t. ground ginger
½ t. cinnamon
½ t. ground cardamom
¼ t. ground cloves

Combine all ingredients in a large bowl; store in an airtight container. Attach gift tag with instructions. Makes 5 cups.

Angie Reedy
Mackinaw, IL

Instructions:

Add ⅓ cup tea mix to ½ cup boiling water in a mug; stir well. Makes one serving.

Copy & attach!

Chai Tea Mix

Instructions:
Add ⅓ cup tea mix to ½ cup boiling water in a mug. Makes 1 serving.

homemade lemonade mix

This summertime favorite is perfect year 'round.

3 c. sugar
1 c. boiling water

3 c. lemon juice
2 T. lemon zest

Combine sugar and water in a stockpot, stirring until sugar dissolves; cool. Add lemon juice and zest; mix well. Cover and refrigerate. Use mix within one week. Attach gift tag with instructions. Makes about 6 cups.

Instructions:

Combine ⅓ cup lemonade mix with ¾ cup cold water; stir well. Makes one serving.

Peppermint
Coffee
Mix

peppermint coffee mix

Tie chocolate-coated Candy Cane Stirrers onto the bags of coffee mix for an extra chocolatey treat.

1⅓ c. sugar
1 c. powdered non-dairy creamer
1 c. instant coffee granules

½ c. baking cocoa
½ c. peppermint candy, crushed
Candy Cane Stirrers

Combine first 4 ingredients in a large bowl. Place in an airtight container; top with crushed candy. Give with Candy Cane Stirrers and attach instructions. Makes about 4 cups.

candy cane stirrers:

A handy stirrer hangs right on the edge of a cocoa mug!

6-oz. pkg. semi-sweet chocolate
   chips, divided

50 mini peppermint candy canes

Microwave ¾ cup chocolate chips in a small microwave-safe bowl on low (50%) for 1½ minutes. Stir chocolate until smooth; microwave 20 more seconds, if necessary. Add remaining chocolate and stir until smooth. Set bowl in a pan of hot water to keep chocolate soft, making sure water does not mix with chocolate.

Dip straight end of each candy cane into chocolate to coat; place on wax paper to cool. Makes 50.

Instructions:

Combine 2 tablespoons mix with ½ cup boiling water; mix well. Makes one serving.

easiest cheese ball

Make 'em mini…just roll into 6 small balls, wrap individually and give with some crackers.

2 (8-oz.) pkgs. cream cheese, softened
2 (8-oz.) pkgs. shredded sharp Cheddar cheese
1-oz. pkg. ranch dressing mix
¼ t. hot pepper sauce
10-oz. pkg. chopped pecans

Combine cream cheese, Cheddar cheese, dressing mix and hot pepper sauce; form into one large ball. Roll ball in chopped pecans to cover. Refrigerate overnight before serving. Serves 12.

a special friend

I have a special friend who's always done favors for me for no special reason. When we met, we were both stay-at-home moms. I went back to work when my oldest child entered college and, needless to say, I didn't have the time to put into meal preparation as I had before.

One hectic night, my friend showed up on my doorstep. There was no special occasion…she just said she was thinking about me. Though her company was always welcome, she'd brought along a freshly baked pie, my family's favorite! Now that's a special friend.

Judy Bozarth
Fort Wayne, IN

creamy artichoke spread

This spread is always a party pleaser. Be sure to make extra for your hostess!

2 (8-oz.) pkgs. cream cheese,
   softened
2 t. garlic, chopped
1½ t. salt
14-oz. can artichoke hearts, drained
   and chopped

⅓ c. sliced black olives
7 green onions, chopped
6 T. sun-dried tomatoes, chopped
¼ c. fresh parsley, chopped
1 t. fresh chives, chopped

Combine cream cheese, garlic and salt in a medium bowl; stir in artichoke hearts and olives. Add green onions and remaining ingredients, stirring gently. Refrigerate overnight. Serves 6.

creative containers

Line a small flowerpot with parchment paper and fill with Creamy Artichoke Spread. Place it in a larger flowerpot and fill the gap with ice cubes…the spread will stay cold while you transport it to a friend or neighbor.

pear honey

Most people with pear trees will gladly share their harvests. Return the favor with a jar of this sweet honey.

8 lbs. pears, cored and peeled
6 lbs. sugar
1 T. butter

20-oz. can crushed pineapple
16 (½-pt.) canning jars and lids, sterilized

Grate pears; place in a large heavy saucepan. Add sugar and butter; mix well. Bring to a boil; boil gently 2 hours. Stir in pineapple; boil 5 more minutes. Spoon into hot sterilized jars, leaving ¼-inch headspace. Remove air bubbles; wipe jar rims. Cover at once with metal lids and screw on bands. Process in a boiling water bath 10 minutes; set jars on a towel to cool. Makes 16 jars.

Ann Rennier
Columbia, MO

"Handed down for generations, this recipe is a favorite spooned on homemade bread or biscuits."

Ann

strawberry freezer jam

Spread this jam over biscuits or a toasted slice of Farmhouse Honey-Wheat Bread (page 227) for your morning breakfast. If the jam is frozen, let it thaw overnight in your refrigerator and stir it before serving.

2 c. strawberries, hulled and crushed
4 c. sugar
1¾-oz. pkg. powdered pectin

¾ c. water
5 (½-pt.) freezer-safe airtight plastic containers, sterilized

Combine strawberries and sugar in a large mixing bowl; set aside.

Whisk together pectin and water in a small saucepan; bring to a boil. Boil, stirring constantly, one minute; remove from heat. Pour pectin mixture over strawberry mixture; stir until sugar dissolves, about 3 minutes.

Spoon into containers leaving ½-inch headspace and secure lids. Set aside in refrigerator until set, up to 24 hours. Freeze up to one year. Makes 5 containers.

Connie Bryant
Topeka, KS

champagne mustard

This tasty gift is sure to delight any hostess when it's packed along with seasoned toasts or crunchy bagel chips.

⅔ c. dry mustard
⅔ c. champagne vinegar
3 eggs

¾ c. sugar
½ t. dried tarragon or dried basil

Whisk together mustard and vinegar; whisk in eggs and sugar. Pour into a heavy saucepan; cook, stirring constantly, until thickened. Remove from heat; stir in tarragon or basil. Spoon into an airtight container. Refrigerate up to one week. Makes about 2 cups.

celebrate!

Use a paint marker to write "Happy New Year" on an ice bucket filled with a jar of Champagne Mustard, breadsticks for dipping, noisemakers and confetti…a ready-made celebration!

all-pasta sauce

One taste of this homemade pasta sauce, and you won't be tempted to use the store-bought sauce again! Use in place of tomato or spaghetti sauce all year long.

11 lbs. tomatoes, chopped
2 green peppers, chopped
1½ lbs. onions, chopped
24-oz. can tomato paste
1 c. vegetable oil
¾ c. sugar
¼ c. canning salt
2 cloves garlic, chopped

2 bay leaves
1½ T. dried basil
1 T. dried parsley
½ T. dried oregano
4 (1-qt.) canning jars and lids,
    sterilized
¼ c. balsamic vinegar, divided

Process tomatoes, green peppers and onions in batches in a blender; add to a large stockpot. Bring to a boil; boil gently for one hour. Stir in tomato paste and next 8 ingredients; boil one more hour. Remove and discard bay leaves.

Spoon into hot sterilized jars, leaving ½-inch headspace. Add one table-spoon balsamic vinegar to each jar. Remove air bubbles; wipe jar rims. Cover at once with metal lids and screw on bands. Process in a boiling water bath 20 minutes; set jars on a towel to cool. Makes 4 jars.

Vickie
Gooseberry Patch

best-dad-in-the-land barbecue rub

Rub about ⅓ cup of this mix onto beef brisket at least 2 hours before cooking…an easy mix to add to a Fathers' Day grilling gift.

16-oz. bottle seasoned salt
1 c. brown sugar, packed
⅔ c. chili powder
¼ c. paprika
2 T. garlic salt
1½ T. pepper

2 t. dry mustard
1 t. ground ginger
1 t. ground nutmeg
1 t. ground cloves
1 t. mesquite-flavored seasoning mix

Combine all ingredients in a mixing bowl; stir well. Store in an airtight container in a dry, cool place for up to 6 weeks. Makes about 3 cups.

happy fathers' day!

Pick up a photo tube at any camera shop and slip this spicy barbecue rub into it. Make a black & white photocopy of one of Dad's favorite photos, scale it to fit the tube and secure with spray adhesive. He'll love it!

backyard-barbecue mango chutney

Add this chutney to your menu for your next outdoor barbecue party. It's so tasty on chicken, pork chops and even fish!

6 c. sugar

6 c. brown sugar, packed

3 c. white vinegar

1½ T. allspice

2 t. cinnamon

2 t. ground ginger

2 t. ground nutmeg

1½ t. ground cloves

1 t. kosher salt

4 red hot chili peppers, seeded and
   chopped

2 onions, chopped

3 cloves garlic, chopped

1 c. golden raisins

1 c. raisins

16 c. mangoes, peeled and sliced

½ c. sliced almonds

4 (1-qt.) canning jars and lids,
   sterilized

Combine first 10 ingredients in a large saucepan; bring to a boil and boil 30 minutes. Add onions, garlic, golden raisins and raisins; boil 30 more minutes. Reduce heat; stir in mangoes and almonds. Simmer 30 minutes; pour into jars, leaving ½-inch headspace. Remove air bubbles; wipe jar rims. Cover at once with metal lids and screw on bands. Store in refrigerator. Makes 4 jars.

for the grilling enthusiast

A jar of fresh Backyard-Barbecue Mango Chutney makes a nice gift for a griller…add tongs, an oven mitt and a grill brush.

caramel apples

It's just not October without these chewy, sweet treats! Keep 'em around for snacks or hand them out as party favors during a fall festival.

2 (14-oz.) pkgs. caramels,
    unwrapped
1½ t. vanilla extract

2 T. water
9 wooden craft sticks
9 tart apples, washed and patted dry

Combine caramels, vanilla and water in a heavy saucepan; cook, stirring constantly, over medium heat until caramels melt. Cool slightly.

Insert craft sticks into apples; dip apples in caramel mixture. Place on a buttered, wax paper-lined baking sheet; refrigerate until firm. Makes 9.

fall treats

After wrapping each apple in cellophane, nestle it inside a small orange gift sack. Add a pumpkin face to the sack using a black permanent marker, then gather the sack around the stick and tie on green curling ribbon.

frosted pecans

Candied pecans are a welcome treat any time of year. Make someone's day with a batch of these goodies.

1½ c. sugar
½ c. sour cream

1½ t. vanilla extract
1 lb. pecan pieces

Combine sugar and sour cream in a large saucepan; bring to a boil over medium heat and simmer, stirring constantly, 5 minutes. Add vanilla and pecans; stir until pecans are well coated.

Spread on wax paper; break into pieces when cool. Store in an airtight container. Makes 4 to 5 cups.

Lisa Johnson
Hallsville, TX

chocolate-peanut popcorn

Satisfy your savory & sweet cravings with a batch of this popcorn…all you need with this is a good movie!

12 c. popped popcorn or 2.9-oz. bag microwave popcorn, popped
2¼ c. salted peanuts
1¾ c. milk chocolate chips
½ c. corn syrup
¼ c. butter

Combine popcorn and nuts in a lightly greased roasting pan; set aside. Combine chocolate chips, corn syrup and butter in a heavy saucepan; cook, stirring constantly, until chips and butter melt. Bring mixture to a boil; pour over popcorn mixture, tossing well to coat.

Bake at 300 degrees for 30 minutes, stirring every 10 minutes. Remove from oven; stir and allow to cool slightly in pan. Remove popcorn to a baking sheet lined with lightly greased wax paper to cool completely. Store in an airtight container. Makes 11 cups.

patchwork soup mix

Add a bag of Herbed Oyster Crackers to go along with this hearty soup mix. The pair offers just the right combination for chasing the chill away!

⅓ c. dried yellow split peas

⅓ c. dried green split peas

⅓ c. dried lima beans

⅓ c. dried pinto beans

⅓ c. dried kidney beans

⅓ c. dried Great Northern beans

¼ c. dried minced onion

1 T. chicken bouillon granules

¼ t. ground cumin

¼ t. garlic powder

¼ t. pepper

⅛ t. dried oregano

Herbed Oyster Crackers

Combine all ingredients except crackers in an airtight container. Give with Herbed Oyster Crackers and attach instructions. Makes 2 cups.

herbed oyster crackers:

2 (10-oz.) pkgs. oyster crackers

1 c. vegetable oil

1½ T. ranch dressing mix

1 t. garlic salt

1 t. lemon-pepper seasoning

1 t. dried dill weed

Toss together crackers and oil until completely coated. Add dressing mix and remaining 3 ingredients, stirring well. Spread in a single layer on an ungreased baking sheet; bake at 250 degrees for 10 minutes. Store in an airtight container. Makes 10 cups.

Instructions:

Combine 8 cups water and soup mix in a large stockpot; bring to a boil. Cover, remove from heat and let sit one hour.

Return pan to heat; stir in 2 cups chopped carrots and 1½ cups chopped celery. Add 1½ pounds smoked ham hock; bring to a boil. Cover, reduce heat and simmer 2 hours or until beans are tender; skim fat as necessary. Remove ham hock from soup; remove meat from bone. Chop meat and return to soup. Stir in ¼ teaspoon pepper. Heat thoroughly and serve. Serves 10.

painted desert chili in a jar

The painted desert effect comes from the rippled appearance, like sand art. Bring out the beautiful colors by spooning each ingredient around the edges of the jar, then filling the center.

¼ c. plus 2 T. dried parsley, divided
¼ c. dried minced garlic, divided
1.25-oz. pkg. taco seasoning mix, divided
2 T. dried minced onion
2 T. ground cumin
2 T. paprika

2 T. white cornmeal
2 T. chili powder
1 c. dried pinto beans
¼ c. dried navy beans
¼ c. dried black beans
1 c. dried kidney beans

Layer ingredients in a one-quart, wide-mouth jar as follows: ¼ cup parsley, 2 tablespoons garlic, 2 tablespoons taco seasoning mix, onion, 2 tablespoons taco seasoning mix, cumin, paprika, cornmeal, remaining taco seasoning mix, remaining garlic, chili powder, remaining parsley, pinto beans, navy beans, black beans and kidney beans. Attach instructions.

Instructions:

Cook 2 pounds ground beef in a 12-quart stockpot, stirring until beef crumbles and is no longer pink; drain. Add contents of jar, ¾ cup chopped onion, 4 (14½-ounce) cans diced tomatoes, 12-ounce can tomato paste, ½ cup cider vinegar, ½ cup packed brown sugar, 46-ounce bottle tomato juice and 10 cups water to ground beef in stockpot. Bring to a boil; reduce heat and simmer, partially covered, 2½ to 3 hours, stirring occasionally. Add salt and pepper to taste. Serves 12.

Amy Conrad
Enid, OK

nutty ginger rice mix

Sometimes thoughtful notes are the best way to keep in touch. This cinnamony rice mix is a sweet addition tucked into a gift box with card-making supplies. See our suggestions for making the box below the recipe.

1 c. long-grain rice, uncooked
½ c. roasted peanuts
1 t. cinnamon

1 t. ground ginger
1 cube chicken bouillon, crumbled

Combine all ingredients in a medium bowl; place in an airtight container. Seal and attach instructions. Makes 1½ cups.

Instructions:

Combine 2 cups water, ¼ cup butter and ¼ cup honey in a saucepan; bring to a boil. Reduce heat; add rice mix, cover and simmer 20 minutes. Serves 6.

made by hand

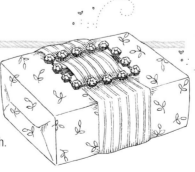

Fill a mini box with all the essentials for making handmade cards…scraps of vintage floral fabrics, buttons, colorful card stock, ribbon, a glue stick, envelopes and stamps. Tie up this pretty package with a ribbon threaded through a decorative buckle or brooch.

cappuccino waffle mix with coffee syrup

Give this mix along with a jar of Coffee Syrup. They'll be a welcome eye-opener for breakfast!

1⅓ c. all-purpose flour

⅓ c. powdered milk

⅓ c. powdered non-dairy creamer

2 t. baking powder

½ t. salt

2 T. instant coffee granules

½ t. cinnamon

Coffee Syrup

Combine first 5 ingredients in a medium bowl. Combine coffee granules and cinnamon in a small bowl. Spoon half of flour mixture into a pint-size jar.

Layer coffee mixture over flour mixture. Spoon remaining flour mixture over coffee mixture. Seal container. Give with Coffee Syrup and attach instructions. Makes 2 cups.

coffee syrup:

1 c. brewed coffee

2 c. sugar

Combine both ingredients in a heavy saucepan; cook over medium-high heat, stirring constantly, until sugar dissolves. Bring to a boil, without stirring; boil 2 minutes. Remove from heat; cool to room temperature. Store in an airtight container in the refrigerator. Makes 1¾ cups.

Instructions:

Beat ½ cup softened butter, one cup sugar and 1½ teaspoons vanilla extract at medium speed with an electric mixer until creamy. Gradually blend butter mixture into waffle mix with a pastry blender or 2 forks until crumbly. Place mixture in a mixing bowl; add ¾ cup water and 2 eggs, stirring until just combined. Bake according to waffle iron manufacturer's directions. Serve with warm Coffee Syrup. Makes 5 to 6 waffles.

take-a-break mocha muffin mix

Surprise a good friend with a special gift of this muffin mix…just because.

1¾ c. all-purpose flour
¾ c. plus 1 T. sugar, divided
2 T. plus ½ t. baking cocoa, divided
2½ t. baking powder

2 t. instant coffee granules
½ t. salt
½ c. mini chocolate chips

Stir together flour, ¾ cup sugar, 2 tablespoons baking cocoa, baking powder, coffee granules and salt. Spoon into a one-quart jar; set aside. Place chocolate chips in a small plastic zipping bag; seal and place on top of mix. Place remaining one tablespoon sugar and remaining ½ teaspoon cocoa in a mini plastic zipping bag; place in jar. Secure lid; attach instructions. Makes 3 cups.

Instructions:

Combine muffin mix with one cup milk, ½ cup melted butter, one beaten egg and one teaspoon vanilla extract; mix until just moistened. Fold in chocolate chips; spoon equally into 12 greased or paper-lined muffin cups. Sprinkle with sugar-cocoa mixture in small packet; bake at 375 degrees for 15 to 18 minutes. Cool on a wire rack. Makes one dozen.

box of love

Tell a best friend no one else can fill her shoes! Cover the lid of a plain shoe box with pictures of shoes cut from magazines or catalogs. Fill the box with bags of the muffin mix, chocolate chips and the sugar-cocoa topping; wrap the box with pretty cotton string.

terrific truffle cake mix

Show appreciation for the friends next door by giving them this chocolatey mix on Good Neighbor Day. It's always the fourth Sunday in September.

3 c. all-purpose flour

3 c. sugar

½ c. baking cocoa

1 t. baking soda

½ t. vanilla powder

Combine all ingredients; place in a plastic zipping bag. Attach instructions. Makes 6½ cups.

Instructions:

Beat ¾ cup softened butter at medium speed with an electric mixer until creamy; add 5 eggs, one at a time, mixing well after each addition. Add one cup milk; mix well. Add cake mix; beat 3 minutes. Pour into a greased 9-cup Bundt® pan; bake at 325 degrees for 60 to 70 minutes or until an inserted toothpick in center comes out clean. Cool in pan 25 minutes on a wire rack; remove from pan and cool completely on wire rack. Serves 15 to 18.

good neighbor surprise

Make a cone shape from pretty scrapbook paper. Glue in place. Punch a hole in each side of the cone and slide ribbon or rick rack through to make a handle; tie each end to secure. Place a bag filled with your favorite goodies into the cone. Slipped over a doorknob, it's sure to be a welcome Good Neighbor Day surprise!

brownies baked in a jar

Slide these brownies out of their jars, slice and enjoy with scoops of your favorite ice cream and chocolate sauce. Be sure to use wide-mouth jars, or the brownies can't slide out!

1 c. all-purpose flour
1 c. sugar
½ t. baking soda
¼ t. cinnamon
⅓ c. butter, softened
¼ c. water

¼ c. buttermilk, room temperature
3 T. baking cocoa
½ t. vanilla extract
1 egg, beaten
3 (1-pt.) wide-mouth canning jars
    and lids, sterilized

Combine first 4 ingredients in a medium bowl. Beat butter at medium speed with an electric mixer until creamy; add water and next 4 ingredients, beating until combined. Add flour mixture, mixing until just blended. Divide batter equally among buttered jars; wipe rims. Each jar should be slightly less than half full.

Place jars on a jelly-roll pan in center of oven; bake, uncovered, at 325 degrees for 40 minutes. Wipe rims; cover with metal lids and screw on bands. Set aside to cool. Makes 3 pints.

an ooey-gooey treat

Give Brownies Baked in a Jar with whimsical sundae dishes, colorful spoons and a sampling of ice-cream toppings…a treat to beat the summer heat!

white chocolate fudge

No candy thermometer needed for this quick fudge! You can make it in less than 25 minutes.

6 oz. premium white chocolate, chopped
½ (8-oz.) pkg. cream cheese, softened

3 c. sifted powdered sugar
½ t. vanilla extract
1 c. chopped pecans
25 pecan halves

Place white chocolate in top of a double boiler; bring water to a boil. Reduce heat to low; cook until white chocolate melts, stirring occasionally. Remove from heat.

Beat cream cheese at high speed with an electric mixer until creamy. Gradually add sugar; beat at medium speed until smooth. Stir in melted white chocolate and vanilla; beat well. Stir in chopped pecans.

Press mixture into a lightly buttered 8"x8" pan. Cover and chill. Cut into squares. Gently press a pecan half on each square of fudge. Store in an airtight container in the refrigerator. Makes 25 squares (1½ pounds).

master cookie mix

(pictured on page 272)

Attach a gift card with recipes for Coconut Bites and Best Chocolate Chip Cookies...this mix makes both flavors of cookies!

5 c. all-purpose flour
3¾ c. sugar
2 T. baking powder

1½ t. salt
1½ c. plus 2 T. butter, softened

Combine flour, sugar, baking powder and salt in a large bowl. Cut in butter with a pastry blender or 2 forks until mixture resembles coarse crumbs. Store in an airtight container in the refrigerator. Attach recipes. Makes 11½ cups.

coconut bites:

3 c. Master Cookie Mix
2 eggs
1 T. lemon zest
1 c. flaked coconut

¾ c. chopped pecans
½ c. red candied cherries, chopped
Garnish: sugar

Beat cookie mix, eggs and lemon zest at medium speed with an electric mixer until combined; stir in coconut, pecans and cherries. Spread mixture in a well-greased 13"x9" baking pan. Bake at 350 degrees for 20 to 25 minutes or until center springs back when lightly pressed. Sprinkle with sugar while warm, if desired; cool and cut into squares. Makes 4 dozen.

best chocolate chip cookies:

2 c. Master Cookie Mix
½ c. brown sugar, packed
1 egg

1 t. vanilla extract
1 c. semi-sweet chocolate chips
½ c. chopped walnuts

Beat cookie mix, brown sugar, egg and vanilla at medium speed with an electric mixer until combined; stir in chocolate chips and nuts. Drop by rounded teaspoonfuls onto greased baking sheets. Bake at 375 degrees for 12 to 15 minutes or until golden; cool on wire racks. Makes 3 dozen.

happy birthday cookies

With alphabet cookie cutters, you can spell out a greeting or a friend's name for a birthday surprise!

¾ c. butter, softened
1 c. powdered sugar
1 egg
1½ t. almond extract

4 c. all-purpose flour
⅛ t. salt
Icing
colored sprinkles

Beat butter and sugar at medium speed with an electric mixer until creamy. Add egg and almond extract; beat until smooth. Combine flour and salt in a separate bowl; add to butter mixture, stirring until a soft dough forms. Divide dough in half; wrap in plastic wrap and chill one hour.

Roll dough to ¼-inch thickness on a lightly floured surface. Use alphabet cookie cutters to cut out "happy birthday" cookies; place on greased baking sheets. Bake at 350 degrees for 8 to 10 minutes; cool on wire racks with wax paper underneath racks. Spoon Icing over letters and top with colored sprinkles. Makes 3 to 5 sets of cookies.

icing:

¼ c. water
2 T. corn syrup
4 c. powdered sugar

1¼ t. almond extract
2 to 3 t. whipping cream

Combine water and corn syrup in a heavy saucepan. Add sugar, stirring until well blended; use a pastry brush to scrape down any sugar on sides of pan. Cook over low to medium heat until a candy thermometer registers 100 degrees; remove from heat. Stir in almond extract and 2 teaspoons cream; cool 5 minutes. Add enough remaining cream to make desired consistency. Makes about one cup.

menus *of spring*

family night

serves 8 to 10

Momma's Divine Divan
(page 109)

*Grandma Lucy's Corn
Fritters (page 147)

Cream Cheese Bar Cookies
(page 265)

lunch with friends

serves 3 to 4

Chicken, Artichoke &
Rice Salad (page 196)

Raspberry Scones
(page 211)

Glazed Strawberry Tart
(page 253)

*Double recipe.

celebrate spring!

serves 12

*Praline Mustard-Glazed Ham
(page 72)*

**Asparagus with Tomato
Vinaigrette (page 132)*

*Blue Cheese Potato Salad
(page 201)*

Carrot Cake (page 239)

company's coming

serves 4

Lemony Pork Piccata (page 116)

*Cracked Pepper Linguine
(page 148)*

Gruyère Rolls (page 225)

Friendship Delight (page 234)

menus *of summer*

from the garden

serves 4 to 6

Garlic & Lemon Roasted Chicken
(page 56)

Green Bean Salad with Feta
(page 200)

summertime celebration

serves 8

*Lime & Ginger Grilled Salmon
(page 53)

Company Rice (page 157)

Green Beans Amandine
(page 137)

*Double recipe.

southern supper

serves 4

Dixie Fried Chicken (page 55)

Squash Casserole (page 161)

Roasted Corn with Rosemary Butter (page 145)

Red Velvet Cake (page 243)

fiesta time!

serves 6

Chicken Burritos (page 108)

Cuban Black Beans (page 136)

Garden-Fresh Salsa (page 25)

**Mexican Coffee (page 10)

**Quadruple recipe.

menus *of fall*

cozy supper

serves 6

*Maple-Curry Pork Roast
(page 65)*

*Mom's Red Cabbage
(page 144)*

Creamed Peas (page 152)

game-day huddle

serves 6 to 8

The Cheesy Bowl (page 31)

*Blue-Ribbon Chicken Fingers
(page 42)*

*Celebration Snack Mix
(page 18)*

*Peanut Butter Jumbos
(page 262)*

for the guys

serves 8

Italian Sausage Sandwiches
(page 184)

Ice Box Brownies
(page 263)

slow-cooked supper

serves 6

Slow-Cooker Beef Stroganoff
(page 84)

Peppery Biscuit Sticks
(page 206)

menus
of winter

chili night

serves 6

Creamy White Chili
(page 173)

Fiesta Cornbread
(page 207)

easy holiday dinner

serves 6

Pepper-Crusted Roast Beef
(page 88)

Risotto in the Microwave
(page 156)

Broccoli Parmesan *(page 133)*

Honey-Crunch Pecan Pie
(page 247)

winter
warm-up

serves 4 to 6

Chicken Stew with Biscuits
(page 176)

White Texas Sheet Cake
(page 242)

breakfast for
supper

serves 6

Country-Style Supper Skillet
(page 92)

Buttermilk Doughnuts
(page 215)

handy tips *for entertaining*

Stress-Free Party Planning

Make entertaining a breeze with our quick & easy suggestions for no-fuss events.

• **Plan ahead.** Anything that can be done before the party will make things much easier on the day of the party. Nothing makes guests feel more at ease than a relaxed hostess.

• **Create simple centerpieces.** Oh-so simple… the prettiest centerpieces can be created in just minutes. Candles tucked inside a Mason jar and flowers inside an ironstone pitcher are such easy-to-create ideas. Check out other fun suggestions in the tip box on the facing page.

• **Follow an easy menu plan.** Beginning on page 306, we've given you lots of ideas for menus, no matter what the season. Or create your own menus using the recipes within this book. Be creative…host a lunch, a family reunion or an afternoon plant swap and brunch with girlfriends.

• **Remember the little touches.** Fresh flowers and scented candles always add a nice feel in any room of your house.

• **Keep it simple and have fun!** You can still host a wonderful get-together and not spend a lot of time in the kitchen. See our tips on the facing page for inspiring no-cook appetizers.

• **In the unlikely event of leftovers…**our Country Friends® like to send each guest home with a paper tote bag that has a pinwheel tied to the handle and a little "thank you" surprise inside.

countdown to party time

Follow this time line to make entertaining a breeze.

Four to six weeks ahead:
• Set the date and time.
• Make your guest list.
• Plan your menu.
• Select invitations (if using them).

Three weeks ahead:
• Mail holiday invitations. For informal events, mailing invitations two weeks in advance is fine.

One to two weeks ahead:
• Check your supply of chairs, serving dishes, flatware and glassware.
• Make your grocery list; shop for nonperishables.
• Add welcome touches to the front porch.

no-cook appetizers

- Dress up a softened block of cream cheese with colorful hot pepper jelly.

- Serve salsa and chips.

- Pick up chicken fingers from the deli or your favorite restaurant and serve with honey mustard, ranch, honey or sweet & sour sauce.

- Offer different selections of cheese and bread and arrange on a plate or in a basket. Add grapes, apples and other fruits to serve alongside the cheese.

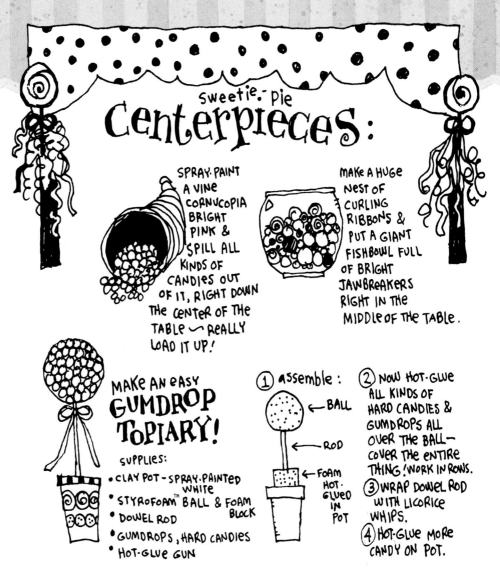

sweetie-pie Centerpieces:

SPRAY-PAINT A VINE CORNUCOPIA BRIGHT PINK & SPILL ALL KINDS OF CANDIES OUT OF IT, RIGHT DOWN THE CENTER OF THE TABLE ~ REALLY LOAD IT UP!

MAKE A HUGE NEST OF CURLING RIBBONS & PUT A GIANT FISHBOWL FULL OF BRIGHT JAWBREAKERS RIGHT IN THE MIDDLE OF THE TABLE.

MAKE AN EASY GUMDROP TOPIARY!

SUPPLIES:
- CLAY POT - SPRAY-PAINTED WHITE
- STYROFOAM™ BALL & FOAM BLOCK
- DOWEL ROD
- GUMDROPS, HARD CANDIES
- HOT-GLUE GUN

① assemble: BALL — ROD — FOAM HOT-GLUED IN POT

② NOW HOT-GLUE ALL KINDS OF HARD CANDIES & GUMDROPS ALL OVER THE BALL — COVER THE ENTIRE THING! WORK IN ROWS.

③ WRAP DOWEL ROD WITH LICORICE WHIPS.

④ HOT-GLUE MORE CANDY ON POT.

Two or three days ahead:
- Get out the china, serving dishes and utensils.
- Shop for perishables.
- Tidy up the house.
- Make place cards (if using them).

One day ahead:
- Plan the centerpiece.
- Prepare any make-ahead dishes.
- Chill beverages. Make extra ice.
- Arrange furniture for best seating and so it's easy to move around.

Day of the event:
- Set the table. Arrange the centerpiece.
- Finish preparing the food and arrange on serving dishes.
- Relax and enjoy your party!

METRIC EQUIVALENTS

The recipes that appear in this cookbook use the standard U.S. method for measuring liquid and dry or solid ingredients (teaspoons, tablespoons, and cups). The information in the following charts is provided to help cooks outside the United States successfully use these recipes. All equivalents are approximate.

METRIC EQUIVALENTS FOR DIFFERENT TYPES OF INGREDIENTS

A standard cup measure of a dry or solid ingredient will vary in weight depending on the type of ingredient.
A standard cup of liquid is the same volume for any type of liquid. Use the following chart when converting standard cup measures to grams (weight) or milliliters (volume).

Standard Cup	Fine Powder (ex. flour)	Grain (ex. rice)	Granular (ex. sugar)	Liquid Solids (ex. butter)	Liquid (ex. milk)
1	140 g	150 g	190 g	200 g	240 ml
¾	105 g	113 g	143 g	150 g	180 ml
⅔	93 g	100 g	125 g	133 g	160 ml
½	70 g	75 g	95 g	100 g	120 ml
⅓	47 g	50 g	63 g	67 g	80 ml
¼	35 g	38 g	48 g	50 g	60 ml
⅛	18 g	19 g	24 g	25 g	30 ml

USEFUL EQUIVALENTS FOR LIQUID INGREDIENTS BY VOLUME

¼ tsp	=						1 ml
½ tsp	=						2 ml
1 tsp	=						5 ml
3 tsp	=	1 tbls		=	½ fl oz	=	15 ml
		2 tbls	= ⅛ cup	=	1 fl oz	=	30 ml
		4 tbls	= ¼ cup	=	2 fl oz	=	60 ml
		5⅓ tbls	= ⅓ cup	=	3 fl oz	=	80 ml
		8 tbls	= ½ cup	=	4 fl oz	=	120 ml
		10⅔ tbls	= ⅔ cup	=	5 fl oz	=	160 ml
		12 tbls	= ¾ cup	=	6 fl oz	=	180 ml
		16 tbls	= 1 cup	=	8 fl oz	=	240 ml
1 pt	=	2 cups	= 16 fl oz	=	480 ml		
1 qt	=	4 cups	= 32 fl oz	=	960 ml		
			33 fl oz	=	1000 ml = 1 liter		

USEFUL EQUIVALENTS FOR DRY INGREDIENTS BY WEIGHT

(To convert ounces to grams, multiply the number of ounces by 30.)

1 oz	=	¹⁄₁₆ lb	=	30 g
4 oz	=	¼ lb	=	120 g
8 oz	=	½ lb	=	240 g
12 oz	=	¾ lb	=	360 g
16 oz	=	1 lb	=	480 g

USEFUL EQUIVALENTS FOR LENGTH

(To convert inches to centimeters, multiply the number of inches by 2.5.)

1 in =		=	2.5 cm	
6 in =	½ ft	=	15 cm	
12 in =	1 ft	=	30 cm	
36 in =	3 ft = 1 yd	=	90 cm	
40 in =		=	100 cm	= 1 meter

USEFUL EQUIVALENTS FOR COOKING/OVEN TEMPERATURES

	Fahrenheit	Celsius	Gas Mark
Freeze Water	32° F	0° C	
Room Temperature	68° F	20° C	
Boil Water	212° F	100° C	
Bake	325° F	160° C	3
	350° F	180° C	4
	375° F	190° C	5
	400° F	200° C	6
	425° F	220° C	7
	450° F	230° C	8
Broil			Grill

index

appetizers & snacks

Antipasto, 29
Apple & Brie Toasts, 33
Asian Gingered Shrimp, 43
Bacon-Wrapped Scallops, 45
Blue-Ribbon Chicken Fingers, 42
Caramel Apples, 289
Celebration Snack Mix, 18
Chocolate-Peanut Popcorn, 291
Cinnamon-Sugar Nuts, 14
Creamy Artichoke Spread, 279
Easiest Cheese Ball, 278
Fried Cheese Sticks, 37
Frosted Pecans, 290
Garden-Fresh Salsa, 25
Grab 'n' Go Gorp, 15
Greek Olive Cups, 41
Greek Spread, 27
Harvest Moon Caramel Corn, 17
Herbed Oyster Crackers, 293
Homemade Tortilla Chips, 25
Maple-Topped Sweet Potato Skins, 38

Parmesan-Artichoke Crostini, 34
Red Pepper Hummus, 26
Smoky Salmon Log, 30
Tasty White Spinach Pizza, 35
The Cheesy Bowl, 31
Turkey-Cranberry Rolls, 39

beverages

Cranberry Slush, 21
Donna's Party Punch, 19
Hot Chocolate Supreme, 13
Iced Coffee, 22
Mexican Coffee, 10
Razzleberry Tea, 23
Spicy Citrus Cider, 11

breads

Apple-Cheddar Bread, 221
Banana-Chocolate Chip Bread, 217
Boston Brown Bread, 222
Braided Coffee Bread, 229
Buttermilk Doughnuts, 215
Cheddar Cheese Spoonbread, 223
Cold Tea Gingerbread, 219
Farmhouse Honey-Wheat Bread, 227
Fiesta Cornbread, 207
Gooey Caramel Rolls, 214
Greek Stuffed Bread, 231
Gruyère Rolls, 225
Lemon Fans, 226
Lemony Apple Muffins, 210
Peaches & Cream French Toast, 213
Peppery Biscuit Sticks, 206

Pineapple-Zucchini Bread, 218
Raspberry Scones, 211
Strawberry Surprise Biscuits, 209
Yankee Bean Pot Bread, 230

cakes

Buttery Pound Cake, 241
Carrot Cake, 239
Double Trouble, 238
Ice-Cream Cone Cakes, 245
Red Velvet Cake, 243
White Texas Sheet Cake, 242

candies & confections

Aunt Mary's Praline Pecans, 267
Candy Bar Fudge, 271
Candy Cane Stirrers, 277
Cola Candy, 270
Rocky Road-Peanut Butter Candy Cups, 269
White Chocolate Fudge, 302

cookies & bars

Baby Cakes, 254
Best Chocolate Chip Cookies, 303
Brownies Baked in a Jar, 301
Brown Sugar Cookies, 255
Chocolatey Pumpkin Cookies, 257
Coconut Bites, 303
Cream Cheese Bar Cookies, 265
Frosted Orange Cookies, 259

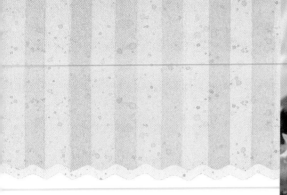

cookies & bars *(continued)*

Happy Birthday Cookies, 305
Ice Box Brownies, 263
Lemon-Oatmeal Bars, 266
Peanut Butter Jumbos, 262
Sugared Pecan Cookies, 258
White Chocolate-Cranberry Cookies, 261

desserts

Friendship Delight, 234
Ice-Cream Tacos, 237
Mom's Apple Dumplings, 235

entrées

Autumn Pork with Apple Chutney, 68
Bacon Florentine Fettuccine, 120
Beef in Rosemary-Mushroom
   Sauce, 80
Cheesy Tuna Tempter, 104
Chicken Burritos, 108
Chicken Chimies, 111
Coconut Shrimp, 49
Country-Style Supper Skillet, 92

Dixie Fried Chicken, 55
Farmhouse Pork & Cabbage Sauté, 71
Fettuccine with Smoked Salmon, 103
Fresh Tomato & Basil Linguine, 100
Garlic & Lemon Roasted Chicken, 56
Gift-Wrapped Chicken, 59
Gobbler Cobbler, 112
Greek Pizza, 97
Green Pepper Steak, 81
Hamburger-Noodle Bake, 124
Ham, Mushroom & Bacon
   Quiche, 93
Hearty Red Beans & Rice, 119
Honeymoon Chicken & Biscuits, 57
Honey-Pecan Pork Cutlets, 117
Italian Stuffed Chicken, 60
Italian 3-Cheese Stuffed Shells, 75
Lasagna Rolls, 77
Lemon-Pepper Fish, 101
Lemony Pork Piccata, 116
Lime & Ginger Grilled Salmon, 53
Linguine & White Clam Sauce, 52
Lucky-7 Mac & Cheese, 96
Maple-Cranberry Turkey, 113
Maple-Curry Pork Roast, 65
Maple-Glazed Turkey Breast, 61
Marinated Brisket, 89
Mexican Lasagna, 79
Mini Meat Loaves, 123
Momma's Divine Divan, 109
Mom's Sicilian Pot Roast, 87
Nacho Grande Casserole, 127
Pepper-Crusted Roast Beef, 88
Perfect Prime Rib, 85

Pork Chops Supreme, 69
Praline Mustard-Glazed Ham, 72
Roast Turkey with Sage Butter, 63
Santa Fe Pork Cutlets, 115
Savory Turkey Loaf, 64
Seafood Lasagna, 48
Shrimp & Wild Rice, 51
Shrimply Divine Casserole, 105
Simply Scrumptious Frittata, 95
Skillet Enchiladas, 129
Slow-Cooker Beef Stroganoff, 84
Spaghetti Pie, 128
Steak & Spinach Pinwheels, 83
Stuffed Cabbage Rolls, 76
Sunday Pork Roast, 67
Tangy Brown Sugar Ham, 121
Thai Peanut Noodles, 107
Vegetable lo Mein à la Rob, 99
Virginia's Baked Spaghetti, 73

frostings, fillings & toppings

Best-Ever Soft Icing, 243
Cola Frosting, 270
Cream Cheese Topping, 265
Creamy Filling, 254
Frosting, 215, 238, 239, 242, 245,
   257, 259
Glaze, 263
Icing, 305
Meringue, 250
Mint Filling, 263

mixes

Angie's Chai Tea Mix, 274
Cappuccino Waffle Mix with Coffee
    Syrup, 297
Homemade Lemonade Mix, 275
Master Cookie Mix, 303
Nutty Ginger Rice Mix, 295
Painted Desert Chili in a Jar, 294
Patchwork Soup Mix, 293
Peppermint Coffee Mix, 277
Take-a-Break Mocha Muffin Mix, 298
Terrific Truffle Cake Mix, 299

pies & pastries

Blackberry Cobbler, 251
Chocolate Sunday Pie, 250
Glazed Strawberry Tart, 253
Honey-Crunch Pecan Pie, 247
Mile-High Lemon Meringue Pie, 249
Peanut Butter & Fudge Pie, 246

salads & dressings

Blue Cheese Potato Salad, 201
Chicken, Artichoke & Rice Salad, 196
Colorful Couscous Salad, 195
Cranberry-Gorgonzola Green
    Salad, 199
Frosty Fruit Salad, 197
Green Bean Salad with Feta, 200
Mediterranean Pasta Salad, 203
Olive Salad, 185
Parmesan-Chicken Salad, 193
The Best Salad, 192

sandwiches

Dressed Oyster Po'boys, 183
French Dip Sandwiches, 188
Giant Meatball Sandwich, 189
Greek Salad in a Pita Pocket, 181
Italian Sausage Sandwiches, 184
Open-Faced Philly Sandwiches, 191
Pepperoni Calzones, 187

Roasted Veggie Panini, 180
Salami Submarine with Olive Salad, 185
Simple Sloppy Joes, 125

sauces & condiments

All-Pasta Sauce, 285
Backyard-Barbecue Mango Chutney, 287
Best-Dad-in-the-Land Barbecue Rub, 286
Champagne Mustard, 283
Chutney, 68
Coffee Syrup, 297
Cream Gravy, 55
Enchilada Sauce, 129
Glaze, 64
Pear Honey, 281
Rémoulade Sauce, 45
Sauce, 99
Strawberry Freezer Jam, 282
Tomato-Basil Sauce, 187

side dishes

Asparagus with Tomato Vinaigrette, 132
Broccoli Parmesan, 133
Calico Beans, 139
Candied-Glazed Baked Apples, 135
Company Rice, 157
Cracked Pepper Linguine, 148
Creamed Peas, 152
Crispy Potato Pancakes, 151
Cuban Black Beans, 136
Dressed-Up Refried Beans, 136
Grandma Lucy's Corn Fritters, 147
Grannie Hobson's Louisiana Red
    Beans, 140
Green Beans Amandine, 137
Honey-Kissed Acorn Squash, 159
Loaded Mashed Potato Casserole, 151
Mom's Red Cabbage, 144
Orange-Maple Glazed Carrots, 143
Praline-Topped Butternut Squash, 160
Rice Pilaf with Carrots, 155
Risotto in the Microwave, 156
Roasted Cauliflower, 141

Roasted Corn with Rosemary Butter, 145
Rosemary Potatoes, 153
Spicy Grilled Vegetables, 164
Squash Casserole, 161
Stuffed Zucchini, 165
Tomato Pie, 163
Vidalia Onion Pie with Mushrooms, 149

soups & stews

Baked Potato Soup, 172
Chicken-Andouille Gumbo, 177
Chicken Fajita Chowder, 171
Chicken Stew with Biscuits, 176
Cream of Chicken-Rice Soup, 169
Creamy White Chili, 173
Curried Harvest Bisque, 168
Mamma Mia Italian Stew, 179
Vegetarian Cincinnati Chili, 175

How did Gooseberry Patch get started?

You may know the story of Gooseberry Patch...the tale of two country friends who decided one day over the backyard fence to try their hands at the mail-order business. Started in Jo Ann's kitchen back in 1984, Vickie & Jo Ann's dream of "A Country Store in Your Mailbox®" has grown and grown to a 96-page catalog with over 400 products, including cookie cutters, Santas, snowmen, gift baskets, angels and our very own line of cookbooks! What an adventure for two country friends!

Through our catalogs and books, Gooseberry Patch has met country friends from all over the world. While sharing our letters and phone calls, we found that our friends love to cook, decorate, garden and craft. We've created Kate, Holly & Mary Elizabeth to represent these devoted friends who live and love the country lifestyle the way we do. They're just like you & me...they're our "Country Friends®!"

Your friends at Gooseberry Patch